GOSPEL SHAPED

WORK

Leader's Guide

GOSPEL SHAPED

WORK

Tom Nelson

THE GOSPEL
COALITION

the good book
COMPANY

Gospel Shaped Work Leader's Guide
© The Gospel Coalition / The Good Book Company 2016

Published by:
The Good Book Company
Tel (US): 866 244 2165
Tel (UK): 0333 123 0880
Email (US): info@thegoodbook.com
Email (UK): info@thegoodbook.co.uk

Websites:
North America: www.thegoodbook.com
UK: www.thegoodbook.co.uk
Australia: www.thegoodbook.com.au
New Zealand: www.thegoodbook.co.nz

ISBN: 9781909919235 Printed in the US

PRODUCTION TEAM:

AUTHOR:
Tom Nelson

**SERIES EDITOR FOR
THE GOSPEL COALITION:**
Collin Hansen

**SERIES EDITOR FOR
THE GOOD BOOK COMPANY:**
Tim Thornborough

**MAIN TEACHING SESSION
DISCUSSIONS:** Alison Mitchell

DAILY DEVOTIONALS:
Carl Laferton

BIBLE STUDIES:
Tim Thornborough

EDITORIAL ASSISTANTS:
Jeff Robinson (TGC), Rachel Jones (TGBC)

VIDEO EDITOR:
Phil Grout

PROJECT ADMINISTRATOR:
Jackie Moralee

EXECUTIVE PRODUCER:
Brad Byrd

DESIGN:
André Parker

CONTENTS

PREFACE

GROWING A GOSPEL SHAPED CHURCH

The Gospel Coalition is a group of pastors and churches in the Reformed heritage who delight in the truth and power of the gospel, and who want the gospel of Christ crucified and resurrected to lie at the center of all we cherish, preach and teach.

We want churches called into existence by the gospel to be shaped by the gospel in their everyday life.

Through our fellowship, conferences, and online and printed media, we have sought to encourage pastors and church leaders to calibrate their lives around what is of first importance—the gospel of Christ. In these resources, we want to provide those same pastors with the tools to excite and equip church members with this mindset.

In our foundation documents, we identified five areas that should mark the lives of believers in a local fellowship:

1. Empowered corporate worship
2. Evangelistic effectiveness
3. Counter-cultural community
4. The integration of faith and work
5. The doing of justice and mercy

We believe that a church utterly committed to winsome and theologically substantial expository preaching, and that lives out the gospel in these areas, will display its commitment to dynamic evangelism, apologetics, and church planting. These gospel-shaped churches will emphasize repentance, personal renewal, holiness, and the wonderful life of the church as the body of Christ. At the same time, there will be engagement with the social structures of ordinary people, and cultural engagement with art, business, scholarship and government. The church will be characterized by firm devotion to the truth on the one hand, and by transparent compassion on the other.

The Gospel Coalition believes in the priority of the local church, and that the local church is the best place to discuss these five ministry drivers and decide how to integrate them into life and mission. So, while being clear on the biblical principles, these resources give space to consider what a genuine expression of a gospel-shaped church looks like for you in the place where God has put you, and with the people he has gathered into fellowship with you.

Through formal teaching sessions, daily Bible devotionals, group Bible studies and the regular preaching ministry, it is our hope and prayer that congregations will grow into maturity, and so honor and glorify our great God and Savior.

Don Carson
President

Tim Keller
Vice President

INTRODUCTION

As gospel-loving people, we say that the gospel influences every dimension of our lives; yet many of us struggle with living out a gospel-shaped faith, particularly when it comes to our work. It is easy and convenient to compartmentalize our lives, worshiping one way on Sunday and working in quite another way on Monday. Are your Sunday faith and your Monday work seemingly worlds apart? Is your Christian faith speaking into what you do in the majority of your life? Are you experiencing a sizeable Sunday to Monday gap? I have good news. God's design and desire for you is to embrace a gospel-shaped faith that closes the gap between your Sunday worship and your Monday work.

The Gospel Coalition is addressing the importance of narrowing the all too common Sunday to Monday gap in their Theological Vision for Ministry, entitled, The Integration of Faith and Work:

> *Christians glorify God not only through the ministry of the Word, but also through their vocations of agriculture, art, business, government, scholarship—all for God's glory and the furtherance of the public good. Too many Christians have learned to seal off their faith-beliefs from the way they work in their vocation. The gospel is seen as a means of finding individual peace and not as the foundation of a worldview—a comprehensive interpretation of reality affecting all that we do. But we have a vision for a church that equips its people to think out the implications of the gospel on how we do carpentry, plumbing, data-entry, nursing, art, business, government, journalism, entertainment, and scholarship. Such a church will not only support Christians' engagement with culture, but will also help them work with distinctiveness, excellence, and accountability in their trades and professions...[1]*

In this curricular journey of exploration, we will address both theologically and practically the Sunday to Monday gap. We desire to guide you to greater understanding of how a more integral Christian faith shapes you as a worker, informs the work you do and influences the workplace you inhabit. In each session you will encounter life-changing truths flowing from Holy Scripture regarding the

---

1 You can read the full text of the statement on page 176 of the Handbook.

paid or unpaid work you are called to do throughout the week. You will become aware in fresh and transforming ways of how you have been created and redeemed with work in mind. Your mind will be challenged and your heart encouraged with a hopeful realism, remembering that the work you do now in this time of redemptive history is both energizing and agonizing, both fulfilling and frustrating. You can anticipate a renewed sense of joy from knowing more fully the biblical truth that one day yet future, you will work without the thorns and thistles that are now an inescapable part of the brokenness of all work. In the mysterious providence of God, you will discover it is in and through the joys and pains of your work that you are called to worship God, be spiritually formed, love your neighbors, live out the gospel and proclaim the gospel to others.

It is my heartfelt and hopeful prayer that as you work through this curriculum, you will increasingly realize how much the gospel speaks into the work you are called to do each and every day. May you gain a greater glimpse of how very much your work matters to God and to others, and may the inspired words of the apostle Paul grace your journey of discovery! "Whatever you do, work heartily, as for the Lord and not for men, knowing that from the Lord you will receive the inheritance as your reward. You are serving the Lord Christ" (Colossians 3:23-24).

Tom Nelson

MAKING THE MOST OF
GOSPEL SHAPED
CHURCH

WHAT GOSPEL SHAPED CHURCH WILL DO FOR YOU

God is in the business of changing people and changing churches. He always does that through his gospel.

Through the gospel he changed us from his enemies to his friends, and through the gospel he brought us into a new family to care for each other and to do his will in the world. The gospel brings life and creates churches.

But the gospel of Jesus, God's Son, our Savior and Lord, isn't merely what begins our Christian life and forms new churches. It is the pattern, and provides the impetus, for all that follows. So Paul wrote to the Colossian church:

> Therefore, as you received Christ Jesus the Lord, so walk in him, rooted and built up in him and established in the faith, just as you were taught, abounding in thanksgiving (Colossians 2:6-7).

"As you received … so walk…" In other words, the secret of growing as a Christian is to continue to reflect upon and build your life on the gospel of the lordship of Jesus Christ. And the secret of growing as a church is to let the gospel inform and energize every single aspect of a church's life, both in what you do and how you do it, from your sermons to young mothers' groups; from your budget decisions and your pastoral care to your buildings maintenance and church bulletins.

Letting the gospel shape a church requires the whole church to be shaped by the gospel. To be, and become, gospel shaped is not a task merely for the senior pastor, or the staff team, or the board of elders. It is something that happens as every member considers the way in which the gospel should continue to shape their walk, and the life of their church.

That is the conviction that lies behind this series of five resources from The Gospel Coalition. It will invite your church members to be part of the way in which you shape your church according to the unchanging gospel, in your particular culture and circumstances. It will excite and equip your whole church to be gospel shaped. It will envision you together, from senior church staff to your newest believer. It will enable you all to own the vision of a gospel-shaped church, striving to teach that gospel to one another and to reach your community with that gospel. As you continue to work out together the implications of the gospel that has saved us, you will be guided into Christian maturity in every area of your lives, both personal and corporate.

This resource is for all kinds of churches: large and small; urban and rural; new plants and long-established congregations; all denominations and none. It is for any congregation that has been given life by the gospel and wants to put the gospel at the center of its life.

You can use the five tracks in any order you like—and you can use as many or as few of them as you wish. If you think your church is lacking in one particular area, it will always be helpful to focus on that for a season. But it is our hope that you will plan to run all five parts of the curriculum with your church—perhaps over a 3- or 4-year time frame. Some tracks may be more like revision and confirmation that you are working well in those areas. Others will open up new areas of service and change that you need to reflect upon. But together they will help you grow into an organic maturity as you reflect on the implications of the gospel in every area of life.

HOW TO MAKE THE MOST OF THIS CURRICULUM

Because the gospel, as it is articulated in the pages of the Bible, should be the foundation of everything we do, this resource is designed to work best if a congregation gives itself over to exploring the themes together as a whole. That means shaping the whole of church life for a season around the theme. The overall aim is to get the DNA of the gospel into the DNA of your church life, structures, practices and people.

So it is vitally important that you involve as many people in your congregation as possible in the process, so that there is a sense that this is a journey that the whole church has embarked upon together. The more you immerse yourselves in this material, the more you will get from it. But equally, all churches are different, and so this material is flexible enough to fit any and every church program and structure—see page 24 for more details.

Here are some other suggestions for how to make the most of this material.

PREPARE

Work through the material in outline with your leadership team and decide which elements best fit where. Will you use the sermon suggestions, or develop a series of your own? Will you teach through the main sessions in Sunday School, or in midweek groups? Will you use the teaching DVD, or give your own talks?

Think about some of the likely pressure points this discussion will create in your congregation. How will you handle in a constructive way any differences of opinion that come out of this? Decide together how you will handle feedback. There will be many opportunities for congregation members to express their ideas and thoughts, and as you invite them to think about your church's life, they will have many suggestions. It will be overwhelming to have everyone emailing or calling the Senior Pastor; but it will be very frustrating if church members feel they are not truly being listened to, and that nothing will really change. So organize a system of feedback from group-discussion leaders and Bible-study leaders; make clear which member of senior staff will collect that feedback; and schedule time as a staff team to listen to your members' thoughts, and pray about and consider them.

There is an online feedback form that could be distributed and used to round off the whole track with your congregation.

PROMOTE

Encourage your congregation to buy into the process by promoting it regularly and building anticipation. Show the trailer at all your church meetings and distribute your own customized version of the bulletin insert (download from www.gospelshapedchurch.org).

Embarking on this course together should be a big deal. Make sure your congregation knows what it might mean for them, and what an opportunity it represents in the life of your whole church; and make sure it sounds like an exciting adventure in faith.

Do involve the whole church. Younger children may not be able to grasp the implications of some things, but certainly those who teach and encourage children of 11 and upwards will be able to adapt the material and outlines here to something that is age appropriate.

PRAY

Pray as a leadership team that the Lord would lead you all into new, exciting ways of serving him.

Encourage the congregation to pray. There are plenty of prompts in the material for this to happen, but do pray at your regular meetings for the Lord's help and guidance as you study, think and discuss together. Building in regular prayer times will help your congregation move together as a fellowship. Prayer connects us to God, but it also connects us to each other, as we address our Father together. And our God "is able to do far more abundantly than all that we ask or think" (Ephesians 3:20) as his people ask him to enable them to grasp, and be shaped by, the love of Christ that is shown to us in his gospel.

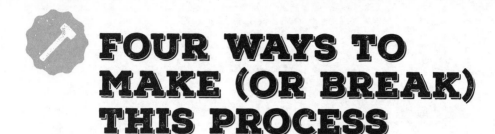

FOUR WAYS TO MAKE (OR BREAK) THIS PROCESS

1. BE OPEN TO CHANGE AS A CHURCH

As churches that love the gospel, we should always be reforming to live more and more in line with that gospel. Change isn't always easy, and is often sacrificial; but it is exciting, and part of the way in which we obey our Lord. Approach this exploration of *Gospel Shaped Work* by encouraging your church to be willing to change where needed.

2. BE OPEN TO CHANGE YOURSELF

This curriculum will lead every member to think hard about how the gospel should shape, and in some ways re-shape, your church. You are giving them permission to suggest making changes. As a leader, giving such permission is both exciting and intimidating. It will *make* your course if you enter it as a leadership excited to see how your church may change and how you may be challenged. It will *break* it if you approach it hoping or expecting that your members will simply agree in every way with what you have already decided.

3. DISCUSS GRACIOUSLY

Keep talking about grace and community. Church is about serving others and giving up "my" own wants, not about meeting "my" own social preferences and musical tastes. Encourage your membership to pursue discussions that are positive, open and non-judgmental, and to be able to disagree lovingly and consider others' feelings before their own, rather than seeking always to "win." Model gospel grace in the way you talk about the gospel of grace.

4. REMEMBER WHO IS IN CHARGE

Jesus Christ is Lord of your church—not the leadership, the elders or the membership. So this whole process needs to be bathed in a prayerful sense of commitment to follow him, and to depend on his strength and guidance for any change his Spirit is prompting. Keep reminding your church that this process is not about becoming the church they want, but the one your Lord wants.

HOW TO USE
GOSPEL SHAPED
WORK

HOW TO USE GOSPEL SHAPED WORK

Gospel Shaped Work is designed to be a flexible resource to fit a wide variety of church settings. The **Main Teaching Session** is the core of the curriculum—the other components grow out of this. The more elements you use, the greater the benefit will be to your church.

The elements of this course are:

- **MAIN TEACHING SESSION** with DVD or talk, and discussion (core)
- **PERSONAL DEVOTIONALS** (recommended)
- **GROUP BIBLE STUDY** (recommended)
- **PERSONAL JOURNAL** (optional)
- **SERMON SERIES** (suggested passages given)

Each church member will need a copy of the *Gospel Shaped Work Handbook*. This contains everything they need to take part in the course, including the discussion questions for the **Main Teaching Session**, **Personal Devotionals**, and the **Group Bible Study**. There's also space to make notes during the sermon, and a **Personal Journal** to keep a record of the things they have been learning.

Each person who will be leading a group discussion, either in the **Main Teaching Session** or the **Group Bible Study**, will need a copy of the *Gospel Shaped Work Leader's Guide*. This includes leader's notes to help them guide a small group through the discussion or Bible-study questions, and other resources to give more background and detail. In the Leader's Guide, all the instructions, questions, comments, prayer points etc. that also appear in the Handbook are in **bold text**.

Further copies of the *Handbook* and *Leader's Guide* are available from **WWW.GOSPELSHAPEDCHURCH.ORG/WORK**

A FLEXIBLE CURRICULUM

Gospel Shaped Work is designed to be a flexible resource. You may be able to give your whole church over to working through it. If so, a typical week might look like this:

SUNDAY
- Adult Sunday school: **Main Teaching Session** using DVD or live talk (talk outline given in *Leader's Guide*)
- Morning service: **Sermon** based on main theme (suggested Bible passages given in the *Leader's Guide*)

MIDWEEK
- Small groups work through the **Group Bible Study**

CHURCH MEMBERS
- Use the **Personal Devotionals** from Monday to Saturday
- Use the **Personal Journal** to record their thoughts, questions and ideas about things they've been learning throughout the week

Or, if you choose to use the curriculum on a midweek basis, it may be like this:

MIDWEEK
- Small groups work through the **Main Teaching Session** using the DVD

CHURCH MEMBERS
- Use the **Personal Devotionals** from Monday to Saturday
- Use the **Personal Journal** to record their thoughts, questions and ideas about things they've been learning throughout the week

Or you can use the components in any other way that suits your church practice.

HOW TO USE EACH ELEMENT

These sample pages from the *Gospel Shaped Work Handbook* show the different elements of the curriculum.

All of the material in this curriculum quotes from and is based on the ESV Bible.

MAIN TEACHING SESSION

- 60 minutes
- Choose between DVD or live talk
- Discussion questions to help group members discuss the DVD/talk and apply it to their own lives and their church
- Guidance for answering the questions is given in the *Leader's Guide*
- Suggestions for praying together

This is the core of the curriculum. It can be run using the *Gospel Shaped Work DVD*, or by giving a live talk. A summary of the talk is included in the *Leader's Guide* (see page 34 for an example). A full editable script can also be downloaded from **www.gospelshapedchurch.org/work/talks**.

In each session, the DVD/talk is split into either two or three sections, each followed by some discussion questions. At the end of the session there are suggestions to help the group pray specifically for each other.

The discussion questions are designed to help church members unpack the teaching they have heard and apply it to their own lives and to the church as a whole. There are not necessarily right and wrong answers to some of the questions, as this will often depend on the context of your own church. Let group members discuss these openly, and apply them to their own situation.

Keep the discussion groups the same each week if possible, with the same leader (who will need a copy of this *Leader's Guide*) for each group, so that relationships are deepened and the discussions can build on those of previous sessions.

PERSONAL DEVOTIONALS

- Six devotionals with each session
- Designed to be started the day after the main teaching session
- Linked with the theme for each teaching session, but based on different Bible passages
- Help church members dig more deeply into the theme on a daily basis

Each session is followed by six personal devotionals that build on the main theme. They are ideal for church members to use between sessions. For example, if you have the main teaching session on a Sunday, church members can then use the devotionals from Monday to Saturday.

These short devotionals can be used in addition to any regular personal Bible study being done by church members. They would also form a useful introduction for anyone trying out personal Bible reading for the first time.

As well as being in the group member's **Handbook**, the personal devotionals are available for a small fee on the Explore Bible Devotional app. This can be downloaded from the iTunes App Store or Google Play (search for "Explore Bible Devotional"). Select "Gospel Shaped Work" from the app's download menu.

PERSONAL JOURNAL

- A useful place for church members to note down what they have been learning throughout the week, and any questions they may have

SERMON NOTES

- If the Sunday sermon series is running as part of **Gospel Shaped Work**, this is a helpful place to make notes

GROUP BIBLE STUDY

- 40 – 50 minutes
- An ideal way for small groups to build on what they have been learning in the main teaching
- Uses a different Bible passage from the DVD/talk
- Suggested answers to the questions are given in the *Leader's Guide*

This study is ideal for a home group or other group to work through together. It builds on the theme covered by the main teaching session, but is based on a different Bible passage. You can see the passages and themes listed in the grid on pages 28-29.

If possible, give 40 – 50 minutes for the Bible study. However, it can be covered in 30 minutes if necessary, and if you keep a close eye on time. If your church is not using the Bible studies as part of a regular group, they would also be suitable for individuals to do on their own or in a pair if they want to do some further study on the themes being looked at in the course.

SERMON SUGGESTIONS

The *Leader's Guide* gives a choice of three sermon suggestions to tie in with each session:

- A passage that is used in the main teaching session (DVD or live talk)
- The Bible reading that is being studied in the Group Bible Study that week
- A third passage that is not being used elsewhere, but that picks up on the same themes. This is the passage that is listed in the overview grid on pages 28-29.

FURTHER READING

At the end of each session in the *Leader's Guide* you will find a page of suggestions for further reading. This gives ideas for books, articles, blog posts, videos, etc. that relate to the session, together with some quotes that you might use in sermons, discussion groups and conversations. Some of these may be helpful in your preparation, as well as helping any group members who want to think more deeply about the topic they've been discussing.

CURRICULUM OUTLINE AT A GLANCE

SESSION	MAIN TEACHING (DVD/TALK)	PERSONAL DEVOTIONS	GROUP BIBLE STUDY	SERMON*
1 **Created to work**	We were created to work, and that is wonderful news. Based on **Genesis 1 and 2**.	Looking at **Psalm 8**, a hymn that helps us enjoy the truths of Genesis 1 and 2.	**Genesis 1:1-31** Helping group members think more deeply about our fundamental attitude toward ourselves and our work.	PSALM 104
2 **Work and the fall**	How to be realistic about the frustration and struggle of our work without being without hope. Based on **Genesis 3**.	Walking through several episodes from **Genesis 4 to 24**, showing the effects of sin on our working lives.	**Luke 12:13-34** Looking at a parable of Jesus that exposes some of our false thinking post-fall, and that has the gospel firmly at its center.	GEN 11:1-9
3 **Renewed work**	Not only will all of God's people be redeemed; all of God's creation will too. This impacts how we view our work. Various passages including **Romans 5 and 8**.	Looking at **Romans 1 – 3**, taking us to the heart of why we need redemption and how God provides it at the cross.	**Exodus 31:1-11** God gives his people his Spirit in order that together they may do the work he calls them to do.	JAMES 1:2-12
4 **Glorifying God through work**	Discipleship is for the whole of life, including our work. Based on **Matthew 11:28-30**.	Studying Paul's words in **Colossians 4:2-6**, looking at how we can live for Christ and speak as his witnesses in our workplaces.	**Colossians 3:1-17** Looking at some of the changes in attitude and lifestyle that come with belonging to Christ.	LUKE 3:1-17

SESSION	MAIN TEACHING (DVD/TALK)	PERSONAL DEVOTIONS	GROUP BIBLE STUDY	SERMON*
5 The gospel and your work	Based on **Philemon**, to see what a first-century relationship between a master and his slave can teach us about work today.	Looking at **1 Peter 2:11-25**, to see how to live in a way that is honorable and causes others to glorify God.	**Colossians 3:22 – 4:1** How Christ transforms our view of work.	EPH 6:5-9
6 Work and power	We all have "vocational power" to influence others and spread *shalom* in the world. Based on **Jeremiah 29:4-14**.	Looking at the life in Babylonian exile of Daniel, Shadrach, Meshach and Abednego in **Daniel 1 – 7**.	**Mark 10:32-45** Looking at Jesus' teaching on how Christians are to use their power and authority.	PROVERBS 31
7 Work and the common good (optional**)	Exploring ideas about economics in the world. Various passages in both Old and New Testaments.	How the gospel transforms our view on and use of money. **Luke 19:1-10** (Zacchaeus) and **1 Timothy 6:6-19**.	**James 4:13 – 5:6** How we choose to spend our time and money.	2 COR 8 – 9
8 What we are working toward	In the new creation work will continue, and work will be better. Based on **Revelation 21 – 22** and **Isaiah 65**.	Looking at **Proverbs**, highlighting what godly wisdom looks like in our day-to-day work.	**Psalm 8; Hebrews 2:5-9** Exploring further that eternity in the new creation is both physical and involves work.	2 TIM 2:8-13

* **Sermon:** The *Leader's Guide* gives three or four sermon suggestions to tie in with each session. Usually, the first picks up a passage from the Main Teaching Session; the second uses the passage from the Group Bible Study; and the third is a new passage, linked with the theme but not used elsewhere in the session. This third passage is the one listed here.

** **Session 7:** This session on economics is optional. Depending on experience, some groups may find that it is too complex; others that it is too basic. Choose whether to include it or not based on the make-up of your particular group.

DOWNLOADS

In addition to the material in this **Leader's Guide**, there are a number of extra downloadable resources and enhancements. You will find all of them listed under the Work track at **www.gospelshapedchurch.org** and on The Good Book Company's website: **www.thegoodbook.com/gsc**.

- **DIGITAL DOWNLOAD OF DVD MATERIAL.** If you have already bought a DVD as part of the **Leader's Kit**, you will have access to a single HD download of the material using the code on the download card. If you want to download additional digital copies, in SD or HD, these can be purchased from The Good Book Company website: **www.thegoodbook.com/gsc**.

- **DVD TRAILERS.** Trailers and promotional pieces for the series as a whole and for the individual tracks can be downloaded for free. Use these trailers to excite your church about being involved in **Gospel Shaped Church**.

- **TALK TRANSCRIPTS.** We're conscious that for some churches and situations, it may be better to deliver your own talk for the main session so that it can be tailored specifically to your people and context. You can download the talk transcript as both a PDF and as an editable Word document.

- **FEEDBACK FORMS.** Because **Gospel Shaped Church** is designed as a whole-church exploration, it's important that you think through carefully how you will handle suggestions and feedback. There's some guidance for that on pages 17-18. We've provided a downloadable feedback form that you can use as part of the way in which you end your time using the resource. Simply print it and distribute it to your church membership to gather their thoughts and ideas, and to get a sense of the issues you may want to focus on for the future. In addition, there are also fully editable versions of this feedback form so that you can create your own customized sheet that works effectively for the way in which you have used this material, and which suits your church membership. Alternatively, you could use the questions to create your own online feedback form with Google Forms or some other software, to make collecting and collating information easier.

- **RESOURCE LIST.** For each session in this *Leader's Guide* we have included a list of resources that will help you in your preparation for sermons, discussions, Bible studies and other conversations. On the *Gospel Shaped Church* website, you will find an up-to-date list of resources, plus a shorter downloadable list that you might consider giving to church members to supplement their own reading and thinking.

- **BULLETIN TEMPLATES.** Enclosed with the *Leader's Kit* is a sample of a bulletin-insert design to promote the Work track to your church. You can download a printable PDF of the design from the *Gospel Shaped Church* website to add your own details, and to print and distribute to your congregation.

- **OTHER PROMOTIONAL MATERIAL.** Editable powerpoint slides and other promotional material to use.

 WWW.GOSPELSHAPEDCHURCH.ORG/WORK

 WWW.THEGOODBOOK.COM/GSC/WORK

SESSION 1:

CREATED TO
WORK

WHY ARE WE HERE? THAT IS OFTEN A SURPRISINGLY
DIFFICULT QUESTION TO ANSWER – AND NOT MANY
OF US WOULD INCLUDE THE WORD "WORK" IN OUR
RESPONSE. IN THIS SESSION, YOU'LL LEARN THAT ONE
OF THE PURPOSES FOR WHICH WE WERE CREATED IS, IN
FACT, TO WORK – AND WHY THAT IS WONDERFUL NEWS.

TALK OUTLINE

1.1 ● Most Christians know the answer to the question "Why did Jesus come?" But many of us struggle with the question: "Why are *we* here?" We must look at Genesis 1– 2.

1.2 ● **MADE TO WORK** *Genesis 1 – 2*
- Why did God make humanity? We are all created to work (1:27-28).
- We are made in God's image—and God is himself a worker.
- The five commands in 1:28 give us a definition of work in three areas...

● **WORK AS CREATION** *Gensis 2:15*
- A central aspect of our creative work is making and raising families (1:28). Raising children is therefore of great significance.
- God tells Adam and Eve to take the garden and expand it into all of creation. Work is creation—the expansion of human flourishing into all of God's creation.

● **WORK AS COLLABORATION**
- **Collaboration with God,** when we work at things which reflect his true nature.
- **Collaboration with others:** Adam needed a co-worker (2:18). Co-operation with others is central to our work.

● **WORK AS CULTIVATION**
To "subdue" and "have dominion" mean that Adam is to harness and **cultivate** the garden's potential. We are to be good **stewards** of the assets God has put under our charge, rearranging God's raw materials so that it helps people to thrive.

1.3 ● **WORK UNDER GOD**
This view of work has three implications:
- There is no such thing as "menial" labor.
- All humans bear God's image when they work—we should honor all workers.
- Your work participates in God's mission.

● **CONCLUSION:** We were made to be workers; and work is fundamentally good.

 You can download a full transcript of these talks at
WWW.GOSPELSHAPEDCHURCH.ORG/WORK/TALKS

CREATED TO WORK

* *Ask the group members to turn to Session 1 on page 13 of the Handbook.*

Discuss

If you went out on the street and asked people the question "Why are we here?" what answers do you think you might get?

> This starter question is to get people thinking and talking about the subject they will meet at the beginning of the DVD: "Why are we here?" There are no wrong answers—it's just a brief, relaxed chat to help break the ice and introduce the theme of the session.

▶ **WATCH DVD 1.1** (3 min 49 sec) **OR DELIVER TALK 1.1** (see page 34)

* *Encourage the group to make notes as they watch the DVD or listen to the talk. There is space for notes on page 15 of the Handbook.*

Discuss

READ GENESIS 1:26 – 2:3

> ²⁶ *Then God said, "Let us make man in our image, after our likeness. And let them have dominion over the fish of the sea and over the birds of the heavens and over the livestock and over all the earth and over every creeping thing that creeps on the earth."*
>
> ²⁷ *So God created man in his own image,*
>   *in the image of God he created him;*
>   *male and female he created them.*
>
> ²⁸ *And God blessed them. And God said to them, "Be fruitful and multiply and fill the earth and subdue it, and have dominion over the fish of the sea and over the birds of the heavens and over every living thing that moves on*

the earth." ²⁹ And God said, "Behold, I have given you every plant yielding seed that is on the face of all the earth, and every tree with seed in its fruit. You shall have them for food. ³⁰ And to every beast of the earth and to every bird of the heavens and to everything that creeps on the earth, everything that has the breath of life, I have given every green plant for food." And it was so. ³¹ And God saw everything that he had made, and behold, it was very good. And there was evening and there was morning, the sixth day.

2 Thus the heavens and the earth were finished, and all the host of them. ² And on the seventh day God finished his work that he had done, and he rested on the seventh day from all his work that he had done. ³ So God blessed the seventh day and made it holy, because on it God rested from all his work that he had done in creation.

In Genesis 1:28, God tells the first people how they are to live. What are the five commands he gives them, and what do they mean?

- *Be fruitful*—primarily to have children, but it implies much more.
- *Multiply*—those children have more children who have more children, and so on, so that the number of people grows.
- *Fill the earth*—spread out so that humans are living all over the earth.
- *Subdue it*—work the earth so that it is fruitful.
- *Have dominion*—rule over the earth.

These ideas will be unpacked later in the session. For now, this question is aiming to ensure that the group understand the basic meaning of each command.

How does this help to answer our opening question: "Why are we here?"

In verse 28, God tells Adam and Eve that they have plenty to do! They are not in the garden just to sit back and relax. They, and their descendants after them, are to work. So right at the beginning of the Bible, God is giving one answer to the question "Why are we here?" We are here to *work*.

Genesis 2:3 tells us that God is a worker. We can also discern one of the reasons why he works—he loves his creation and wants to bless it. He created us in his image (Genesis 1:27), so all humans—as his image bearers—are created to be workers too. Does the idea that you were made to be a worker surprise you? What difference might this truth make on your journey to work, or as you start your day?

Even though this curriculum is on the topic of work, it's likely that some in your group will be surprised to discover that we have all been made to work, especially if their view of work tends to be negative. But God created us to work in Genesis 1—before sin impacted every part of life (in Genesis 3)—so that means that work *is fundamentally good.*

Ask the group whether this view of work as a fundamentally good thing might make a difference to their daily experience. For some it won't. For others, it may lead to a shift in attitude.

NOTE: If group members raise the issue of work being hard, painful, and maybe unfair, explain that we will be thinking about the painful side of work in Session 2.

▶ **WATCH DVD 1.2** (10 min 52 sec) **OR DELIVER TALK 1.2** (see page 34)

* *Encourage the group to make notes as they watch the DVD or listen to the talk. There is space for notes on page 17 of the Handbook.*

Discuss

In this curriculum, we will see that work is more than just what we do each day, or how we pay our way. Work is creation, collaboration and cultivation— whatever our daily occupation, paid or not.

Look at your work (paid or otherwise) through the lens of "work as creation." How does your specific work help to build, create, strengthen or expand human society?

Some group members will find this easy to answer, but others may struggle. If someone finds it hard to recognize any aspect of their own work that "builds, creates, strengthens or expands human society," ask the other members of the group for ideas. Often, someone else can see positives that an individual may miss. Possible answers could include: cleaners making our buildings nicer and safer for human society to flourish in; teachers helping children grow in wisdom and knowledge that will serve human society; retired people caring for their neighbors to strengthen human society in their community; homemakers caring for and teaching children; builders creating new homes for people to flourish in; ministers helping God's church to grow.

Work is primarily cultivation—contributing something to the world. But it is also collaboration in two ways: collaboration with God, and collaboration with each other. Can you see how the work you do (paid or otherwise) is collaboration in one or both of these ways?

In the DVD presentation, Tom Nelson said: *"Our work is a collaboration with God's rule when we work at things that reflect his true nature—his justice, righteousness, peace and beauty."* So we are collaborating with God whenever we serve on a jury to support justice in our society; stand up for honesty and fairness in our workplace; help battling neighbors to find a peaceful solution to their dispute; or create a beautiful garden for others to enjoy.

Our work will be collaboration with others when we work alongside others to build, create, strengthen or expand human society.

Work as cultivation means that we are to grow and steward the raw materials of creation. How does your work take the "raw materials" of God's creation to enhance the lives of others?

(Clarify to your group that the "raw materials" could include physical material, or people, or non-physical material such as ideas, numbers or words.)

As with the previous questions, some group members may find it hard to see how their own work "cultivates the raw materials of creation," in which case ask the rest of the group for suggestions. It may also help to remind the group that the work we do isn't only paid employment. It may be that the work people do outside of their daily job is more clearly linked with cultivation. For example, if they volunteer in any children's or youth work, helping young people to grow and develop; if they use practical skills to help a neighbor decorate a room or mend a fence; if they keep the accounts for a local charity, or write articles for a local newsletter.

▶ **WATCH DVD 1.3** (4 min 14 sec) **OR DELIVER TALK 1.3** (see page 34)

* *Encourage the group to make notes as they watch the DVD or listen to the talk. There is space for notes on page 18 of the Handbook.*

Discuss

"There is no such thing as menial labor." How does this change the way you think about dull tasks you undertake during the day, and/or about people who do the kinds of jobs your society considers "menial"?

Some in your group may have been challenged about how they see their own work, or how they view people in certain jobs. For others, this session may have confirmed their existing view of work as good, no matter how "menial" it may appear.

As we think about work over the next few weeks, what questions about work are you hoping will be answered?

You may want to keep a note of the questions your group comes up with— don't feel you have to answer them right away, since many will be addressed during the next seven sessions, or in the personal daily devotionals or weekly Bible study. It may help to check the list occasionally to see which questions have not yet been answered, and decide whether to build some of them into future group discussions.

Pray

Genesis 1 says that we are created to work and that work is fundamentally good.

Pray that during the course of this curriculum, God will show you any attitudes to work that need to change.

Pray that you will grow as godly workers, who are images of God to the world around you.

DAILY BIBLE DEVOTIONALS

As you finish the session, point group members to the daily devotionals to do at home over the course of the next week. There are six, beginning on page XX, and followed by a page for journaling. This week they work through Psalm 8, a hymn helping us enjoy the truths of Genesis 1–2—who God is and how creation points us to him; and who we are as humans, and what our role in creation is.

SERMONS

OPTION ONE: GENESIS 1:26-31; 2:10-15

Tom bases his DVD presentation on the first two chapters of Genesis, and the Bible study then walks through these chapters in more detail; and you could expand upon it (or sections of it) in a longer sermon.

OPTION TWO: PSALM 104

This passage is not mentioned in this material, but picks up on several of the themes of this session, especially the following:

- God is a worker, who works wisely in (v 24), and rejoices over, all his work (v 31).
- God works both powerfully (v 5-13) and intimately (v 14-22).
- Man works within the creation as God works to sustain his creation (v 23).

OPTION THREE: GALATIANS 5:22

This preaching option is for a series on the fruit of the Spirit, considering each aspect of his fruit and how it might be lived by, and lived out, in work contexts. This week: Love.

If one of your Sunday sermons is to be based on the theme of this session, church members will find a page to write notes on the sermon on page 29 of their Handbooks.

BIBLE STUDY

AIM: The main teaching session intoduced us to the the idea of how the Bible sees our daily work. It had some big ideas: God is a worker; we are made in the image of God; we were created to work; and this "creation mandate" for us as workers is to create, cultivate and co-operate as we fulfill God's command to "fill the earth and subdue it"—to extend God's Eden perfection into the whole world. This Bible Study returns to Genesis 1 to reinforce many of these points, but also asks us to think more deeply about our fundamental attitude toward ourselves and our work. Prepare to be challenged!

Discuss

When the subject of work comes up in conversation, what kinds of attitudes do people show toward work? Is that range of attitudes the same when you discuss work at church with other Christians?

There will be a wide range of views displayed. Don't like to think about it or talk about it! Work is a necessary evil—I live for the weekend; work is brilliant, and I love it; I find it boring and repetitive; I can bear the work because I love being with the people; work is everything to me, because it is where I get my sense of purpose from. You would hope that among Christians you might also hear phrases like: "I am really thankful for my work"; "I love the opportunity to serve others." But perhaps not. You may also hear: "Work is a great place to evangelise others"; and "Work is a part of the fallen world." Don't comment on them for now; just log the answers as interesting.

This first session of *Gospel Shaped Work* has shown us some big ideas that may be unfamiliar to people.
- **How does the Bible first reveal God? As a worker who loves his job!**
- **Why are we here? God created us to work!**
- **What is God's "Creation Mandate" for the world? For humans made in God's image to fill the earth and subdue it.**
- **How are we to fulfill that command? By creating, co-operating and cultivation.**

Let's understand these fundamental truths more deeply as we look again at Genesis 1.

READ GENESIS 1:1-25

²⁰ And God said, "Let the waters swarm with swarms of living creatures, and let birds fly above the earth across the expanse of the heavens."
²¹ So God created the great sea creatures and every living creature that moves, with which the waters swarm, according to their kinds, and every winged bird according to its kind. And God saw that it was good.

1. After God made the heavens and the earth (v 1), what was the earth like (v 2)?

- Without form and void.
- There was darkness.
- God was present in and over the world.

2. *From v 3 onwards* we see God at work. What do we learn about the kind of worker God is from these verses.

- He is a planner: his work of forming the earth is planned in stages.
- He is a builder. Each piece is put together methodically, each day of creating resting on the last.
- He takes his time! We may think six days is quick, but God could have done it in an instant. He didn't.
- He loves his work, and takes great joy and pride in it.
- He is creative in ideas—there is a rich diversity in plants and animal life.
- He creates with glorious complexity. The world is incredibly detailed.
- He rests from work, and takes the opportunity to enjoy it.

3. If you look at creation, what does it tell us about our Creator (see also Romans 1 v 19-20)?

- He is great and has awesome power.
- He created the world to be appreciated for its beauty and wonder.
- You might also say that he has a sense of humour—there are some hilarious creatures he has made with astonishing life cycles.

Additional question: If you had a powerful telescope and a microscope, what might you also understand about God?

 **READ GENESIS 1:26-31**

> ²⁶ *Then God said, "Let us make man in our image, after our likeness. And let them have dominion over the fish of the sea and over the birds of the heavens and over the livestock and over all the earth and over every creeping thing that creeps on the earth."*

4. We are made "in the image of God" (v 27)—who is revealed as a worker in Genesis 1. Go through each of your answers to question 2—which of these aspects of God's character do you see in your own work? Which are you best at? Where might you need to develop?

There will be a large variety of answers to this question, but keep the conversation steered toward the positives. Underline that we are looking this week at work *as it was created by God.* If people in the group take no joy in their work at all, note this for addressing in future sessions.

5. What are the five commands God gives to the whole of humankind in verse 28? How can we see the human race fulfill these commands in general? How can you see aspects of them in the work that you do?

- *Be fruitful.* This is a general idea about work that generates life, wealth, health or wellbeing. We are commanded to be productive in all areas of our lives. In general, humans are incredible at this. We create businesses, homes, communities and countries that flourish and achieve remarkable things.
- *Multiply.* This is fruitfulness applied to having children. The human race has done extremely well at this! Make it clear here that child bearing and rearing is central to God's plan for our working lives. Home-making has a very high status in God's plans for the world.
- *Fill the earth*—spread out so that humans are living all over the earth. Again, we've been great at that.
- *Subdue it.* The call to take what is wild and unruly (see Genesis 1 v 1-2), and order it so that it is productive. This applies to turning rough land into farmland. It equally applies to an administrator or an acountant bringing order to a business, or to a household. We have been brilliant at this as a race: advanced farming, use of natural resources, and building in remote and hostile places.
- *Have dominion.* Like God, to rule over the earth. Any exercise of loving power and nurturing control is in obedience to God's creation command.

6. **How should these truths about our nature and position as people in God's world affect the way we view ourselves? How might it change the way we see others?**

- We are incredibly privileged. We have been given the responsibility to rule the world, and to care for and steward God's precious creation.
- This is something that *all* people have been given—irrespective of whether they call the LORD their Lord.
- We should take our responsibility to rule seriously and humbly. We should create, co-operate and cultivate with seriousness, joy and determination.
- We should recognize and value everyone because of their status.
- We should honor, encourage and applaud anyone who rules—in their family, work, community, or in government—when they fulfill their creation mandate to create and cultivate co-operatively in a way that responsibly stewards God's creation. We can and should do this, even if they are not believers, or if part of what they are doing is flawed or driven by ungodly motives.

NOTE: There may be some in your group who find this idea difficult. We have a tendency to entirely dismiss people because they have a certain belief or a particular policy or attitude. We should be able to sift the good from the bad, and give praise for what honors God, even if other things are less praiseworthy in our estimation.

7. **Think about how you feel as you start work on a Monday morning. Think about common attitudes to work among your friends and colleagues. How might the perspective of Genesis 1 change our view of work—whatever that might be?**

- Our work, even if it is mundane and repetitive, can and must be viewed as worship. We are serving God in it and through it. The act of making a widget, changing a diaper, answering a call, sweeping a floor, planting a seed or sending an email can be—*in and of itself*—an act of worship when it is serving God's call to rule, order and cultivate the world—however we are feeling!
- It may not stop a job being difficult or dull, but invests it with new meaning. We can and should praise God for the privilege of our work, and strive to do it with joy and enthusiasm.
- We should also have a relentless positivity about the work of others. Even if they do not praise God in it, we can praise God *for* it.

8. Think of some practical ways we can honor those who work around us—especially those whose work is often considered routine or "low grade."

- We can get into the habit of thanking people for what they do, and encouraging them in it, especially those who are in jobs that are repetitive and dull by their nature.
- Engage relationally with people who serve us in shops or restaurants.
- Show an interest in what people do during the day. Stay-at-home parents; those who are retired from formal paid work but still engage in all kinds of work around the home, or as volunteers.
- Remind people of the value of their work, and why it is important. Work out some ways in which you might do this for those who may not be Christian, but which might introduce them to the idea of God's gift to them.

Apply

FOR YOURSELF: Do you need to change your fundamental attitude toward work? Have you been guilty of a downbeat attitude toward it that does not honor God? How will you help yourself to think differently about work this week?

FOR YOUR CHURCH: Is talking about work subtly looked down on in your church, as if it is not a fit subject for conversation? How often is work referred to in a positive and constructive way in sermons, Bible studies and other church meetings? How might you cultivate a more positive way to discuss work, and work-related matters in the life of your church?

Pray

FOR YOUR GROUP: Discover what each member of your group actually does work wise. Today, try not to focus on particular problems or difficulties—we will get to that next time!. Instead, give thanks for the work, and the way it contributes to God's creation commands.

FOR YOUR CHURCH: As your church embarks on this series examining what it means to let the gospel shape the way we think about work, pray that you would grow together in seeing more clearly the Lord Jesus Christ, and his perfect work in saving us.

FURTHER READING

The maid who sweeps her kitchen is doing the will of God just as much as the monk who prays—not because she may sing a Christian hymn as she sweeps but because God loves clean floors.
Martin Luther

Far and away the best prize that life offers is the chance to work hard at work worth doing.
Theodore Roosevelt

There is no ordinary work. The work God has called you to do is extraordinary. Don't miss out on God's best by taking an ordinary approach to it.
Tom Nelson

Books

- *Work Matters*, chapter one (Tom Nelson)
- *Every Good Endeavor*, part one (Timothy Keller with Katherine Leary Alsdorf)
- *Work: The Meaning of Your Life* (Lester DeKoster)
- *The First Chapters of Everything* (Alasdair Paine)
- *God's Big Picture* (Vaughan Roberts)

Online

- *Do Executive Jobs Have More Kingdom Value Than Dirty Jobs?* (audio) gospelshapedchurch.org/resources411
- *4 Reasons Why God Wills Work:* gospelshapedchurch.org/resources412
- *God the Great Janitor?* gospelshapedchurch.org/resources413
- *5 Ways to Honor Work in Church Services:* gospelshapedchurch.org/resources414
- *Tim Keller on Why Work Matters* (video): gospelshapedchurch.org/resources415
- *Work is a Glorious Thing:* gospelshapedchurch.org/resources416
- *The TGCvocations column asks practitioners about their jobs and how they integrate faith with work.See www.thegospelcoalition.org/channel/faith-and-work*

LEADER'S REFLECTIONS

SESSION 2:
WORK AND THE FALL

SINCE WE WERE DESIGNED TO KNOW THE JOY OF WORK IN GOD'S CREATION, WHY DO OUR WORKING LIVES OFTEN HAVE AS MUCH FRUSTRATION IN THEM AS THEY DO FULFILLMENT? THIS SESSION WILL SHOW YOU HOW TO BE REALISTIC ABOUT YOUR WORK, WITHOUT BEING HOPELESS IN YOUR WORK.

TALK OUTLINE

2.1 Last session we saw that we are created to be workers—but many of us find work frustrating, difficult and exhausting. Genesis 3 explains why. Here we see:
- **broken creation:** Work becomes hard and is often filled with trouble.
- **broken collaboration (v 16):** We have conflict rather than harmonious cooperation.
- **broken cultivation (v 17):** We cannot produce the results we long for. Our work is beset by disappointments.

2.2 ● REALISTIC WORK IN A BROKEN WORLD

Why is work difficult now? Because without faith in Christ, human beings are not reconciled to God. We see this in the "thorns" we face in our work:
- **Relational conflict**, with every person trying to be their own god.
- **Ethical complexity**. *Give examples.*
- **Injustice**, with people using their power to serve their own ends.
- Work feeling **meaningless**.
- **Workaholism**, as we find our identity and value in our work.
- **Slothfulness**, with people only doing enough to get by.

These thorns have two implications for Christians. First, *we are part of the problem!* We too are sinners, who need to daily repent. Second, *we should be realistic.* No job will fill all our deepest longings. We shouldn't be surprised by difficult days and troubled seasons—and we should be grateful when things work well.

2.3 ● HOPEFUL WORK IN A BROKEN WORLD
- We are not cursed... but the serpent is (v 14). There is good news of hope for humans.
- Our work *will* produce fruit to enjoy, even if it is hard work (v 18).
- The story does not end in Genesis 3—God promises a child to defeat the serpent.

CONCLUSION: Work is frustrating, but there is an end date to the difficulties you experience at work. The Bible's story continues with the birth of the Son, who will reconcile us to God and infuse work with new meaning.

You can download a full transcript of these talks at
WWW.GOSPELSHAPEDCHURCH.ORG/WORK/TALKS

WORK AND THE FALL

* *Ask the group members to turn to Session 2 on page 31 of the Handbook.*

Discuss

What is the most frustrating thing about your daily occupation?

This question applies to whatever a person is most regularly involved in doing day to day, whether that is paid work or not. It also leads into the opening video segment, which starts with some *vox pops*—the views of ordinary people answering this question. Try not to let the discussion turn into a long period of grumbling. It is simply designed to introduce the idea that all work is frustrating—something we will be thinking about in this session.

READ GENESIS 3:1-19

¹ Now the serpent was more crafty than any other beast of the field that the Lord God had made...

▶ **WATCH DVD 2.1** (6 min 33 sec) **OR DELIVER TALK 2.1** (see page 52)

* *Encourage the group to make notes as they watch the video presentation or listen to the talk. There is space for notes on page 33 of the Handbook.*

Discuss

In Session 1 we saw that work is creation, collaboration and cultivation. But, because of sin, work is no longer what it could and should be. Can you think of examples of the following?

- Work as broken creation
- Work as broken collaboration
- Work as broken cultivation

In Session 1, your group was asked to think of some examples of work as creation, collaboration or cultivation (see page 18 of the Handbook); ask them to think back to those suggestions and see if they can see how that work has been spoiled by sin. Examples might include:

- **Work as broken creation:** No sooner does a cleaner finish cleaning a building than people drop litter on the floor or spill coffee on the desks; teachers work hard to help children understand new ideas, but those children may misbehave or be disengaged in lessons; builders create new homes that quickly get covered in graffiti; gardeners grow beautiful flowers in a park that get trampled on and destroyed.
- **Work as broken collaboration:** Instead of standing up for honesty and fairness in our workplace (collaboration with God), we keep quiet when we see people stealing office supplies; instead of helping neighbors who are in conflict to come to a peaceful solution (collaboration with God), we take sides or spread gossip; instead of supporting our colleagues (collaboration with others), we can compete with them or seek to undermine them.
- **Work as broken cultivation:** When we volunteer in a local youth group, they seem to be growing but then turn their backs on everything they've learned; when we help mend a neighbor's fence, it is kicked down (or blown down) overnight; when we write articles for a local newsletter, someone complains to the editor that we are bigoted and intolerant.

"Seasons of fruitfulness are often quickly consumed by times of hardship." **Have you experienced this yourself, or seen it happen elsewhere?**

Even though we may find work frustrating, the reality of life is that we experience *both* joy *and* pain in our daily occupations. This is something we will think more about later in this session. Ask the group for any examples they can think of where work has been fruitful, and full of joy, but that hasn't lasted.

Examples might include: a great working relationship with colleagues that changes when an aggressive new person is brought in, or an existing colleague is made redundant; a neighborhood project that successfully rejuvenates a rundown park, only for the owner to change their mind and sell the land as a parking lot; a family vacation that starts wonderfully, but then the children fight over rooms and refuse to join in with family activities for the rest of the week.

▶ **WATCH DVD 2.2** (7 min 42 sec) **OR DELIVER TALK 2.2** (see page 52)

✻ *Encourage the group to make notes as they watch the DVD or listen to the talk. There is space for notes on page 34 of the Handbook.*

Discuss

"We are not simply victims of the brokenness of our workplace; we are co-conspirators." Can you think of examples from your own job or daily occupation where your sin has had a negative impact on your work or on those you work with?

This is a more personal question, so be ready to start with an answer of your own if no one from the group says anything at first. As with all these questions, help the group to see how it applies to those who do not have paid employment as well as those with paid jobs. With a little prompting, most people will be able to think of at least one example of where their own selfishness, laziness or pride has contributed to the brokenness of their workplace (whether that be the office, factory, store or home).

We should not be surprised that work is marred by the results of the fall. But as Christians we will want to act in a way that honors God. How might a Christian respond to the following?

- **A co-worker who regularly tells inappropriate jokes**
- **A manager who bullies their staff**
- **A colleague who encourages you to work less hard so that you don't "show the rest of us up"**
- **A client who objects to you mentioning your faith**

These questions don't necessarily have easy answers, which is another impact of the fall—at times, it can be hard to see a godly path. Here are some possible discussion points:

- Could you ask the colleague who tells inappropriate jokes to avoid certain subjects (such as racism)? But if he/she doesn't listen, it may be that the best you can do is not join in with any laughter, and change the topic to something more wholesome.

- Talking to the manager who bullies his staff may help him see the unfairness of his actions. If not, are there ways to support the person being bullied (but without this turning into a group moan about the manager!).
- You can explain to a lazy colleague why it is that you believe it's right to work hard at your job. But if they are determined to keep being lazy, it may not be possible to avoid ongoing conflict between you.
- Talking to others about our faith is a biblical command, but that doesn't necessarily mean we have to do it during working hours. Are there other times or ways in which you can speak to your co-workers about your faith without it impinging on work time or annoying your boss?

▶ **WATCH DVD 2.3** (3 min 5 sec) **OR DELIVER TALK 2.3** (see page 52)

✦ *Encourage the group to make notes as they watch the DVD or listen to the talk. There is space for notes on page 36 of the Handbook.*

Discuss

How does Genesis 3 help you understand the frustrations of your workplace?

This question and the next one are an opportunity to sum up the teaching from this session, as well as thinking about the difference Genesis 3 may make to our thinking in the coming week. In the DVD, Tom Nelson sums up the reason for work being so frustrating: *"Work is so difficult because now, apart from Christ, human beings are not reconciled to God. This breach is what has opened a flood of disappointment and frustration into our workplaces."* Point out that understanding this allows us to be realistic about work and unsurprised when things go wrong or we are treated unfairly (or treat others unfairly), and reminds us of the futility of seeking our ultimate satisfaction or approval through our work.

It may help to point the group back to Genesis 3:14-19 to find specific answers to why work is now so hard and frustrating. These verses don't just apply to paid employment, but also to things like childbearing (v 16).

How might Genesis 3 give you hope as you face the frustrations of your work?

Again, point the group back to Genesis 3:14-19 to find the answers. These verses include general joys such as the gift of children (v 16), and plants that bear good crops to eat (v 18)—joys that remain, even in this fallen world. But these verses also point to the greatest hope of all—the offspring of Eve, who will destroy the work of the serpent (v 15). Even while we find work (and the whole of life) frustrating, we can look forward to the new creation, where the curse of the fall will be reversed. In the new creation, when Christ has returned, "death shall be no more, neither shall there be mourning nor crying nor pain any more" (Revelation 21:4). And instead of us being cut off from God's garden, the tree of life will be freely available for all those who know and love Jesus (22:1-3).

Pray

"We are not simply victims of the brokenness of our workplace; we are co-conspirators."

Ask God to forgive you for the times when you have contributed to the brokenness of your workplace. Ask him to help you to change. Ask him too, to help you to apologize and repent to a co-worker if that's needed.

Pray that you will be a light in your workplace, living in such a way that it both pleases God and points people to him.

DAILY BIBLE DEVOTIONALS

Remind group members about the daily devotionals they can do at home over the course of the next week. This week we walk through several episodes from Genesis 4 – 24. Five show the effects of sin on humanity and our working lives. The last shows the blessing of working God's way, even in this fallen world.

SERMONS

OPTION ONE: GENESIS 3

Tom focuses on this passage in his DVD presentation, and you could expand upon it in a longer sermon.

OPTION TWO: LUKE 12:13-34

This is the passage the Bible study is based on (see next page), which could also be expanded upon in a sermon.

OPTION THREE: GENESIS 11:1-9

This passage forms the basis for one day's devotional study, but could be expanded upon in a sermon to show a sinful society at work:
- Here is a creative (v 3), proud and self-centered society (v 4).
- They think highly of themselves; but they are very small to God (v 5).
- God will not allow his work to be thwarted by humanity's decisions to work against him (v 8). Greatness lies in being part of his plans (see Abram in 12:1-4).

OPTION FOUR: GALATIANS 5:22: JOY AT WORK

Church members will find a page to write notes on the sermon on page 49 of their Handbooks.

BIBLE STUDY

AIM: The main teaching session showed how the fall has brought frustration and meaninglessness into our working lives. In this Bible study we think about a parable of Jesus that has the gospel firmly at its center. As well as being a gospel challenge to us, however, it exposes some of the false thinking we can all be infected by post fall.

Discuss

What do you love about your work? What kinds of things do you find frustrating or troubling?

Don't let people go on too long on this! Remind people that the reason that work is both great and grueling is because we are both created and fallen. The world makes sense through the lens of the Bible's understanding of who we are.

We are all affected by the curse of the fall. In the well-known story that Jesus tells, and the teaching that follows, we can discern some false ways of thinking about work that easily influence our attitudes.

☛ READ LUKE 12:13-21

> *15 Take care, and be on your guard against all covetousness, for one's life does not consist in the abundance of his possessions.*

1. **What question prompts Jesus to tell his parable and why does he tell it (v 13-15)? What does Jesus see as the questioner's real problem?**

   - Someone asks him to sort out an inheritance problem.
   - Jesus refuses to act as a judge in the case.
   - Instead he challenges the questioner and the whole crowd about their greed and envy—"covetousness" (v 15).

2. **Look at the details of the story in v 16-19. What qualities does the man show that most people would applaud?**

- There was a great crop and a great harvest.
- The man tackles the problem with foresight and intelligence.
- He makes a plan that will make the most of the harvest. We are left in no doubt that he will achieve it.
- He plans for his retirement.
- He is working hard and diligently so that he can rest, relax and enjoy things in his retirement.

Additional question: Where do you hear sentiments like these, and encouragements to carry them out in the world?

Life insurance and pension sales literature; adverts about lifestyle; "self-improvement" manuals and business motivation speakers.

3. **How would you sum up the man's attitude to work and rest? Can you come up with a couple of mottos that he might use to explain his approach to life?**

- He works hard and uses his good luck, intelligence and drive to create wealth. "The harder I work, the luckier I get."
- He has a goal and he is not afraid to work hard to achieve it. "Plan the work and work the plan." "Follow your dreams."
- He is planning for a retirement that allows him to enjoy the fruit of his hard labor. "You've earned it—enjoy it."

4. **What is his one big mistake? (Clue: What is repeated more than 10 times in v 17-19?) Why does it matter?**

- He is entirely thinking about himself. Personal pronouns "I", "me", "mine" and "myself" are repeated again and again in these verses.
- He thought that life was about wealth. He stored up riches for himself, not God.
- This truly is a foolish way to live—someone who is so wise about this life, and yet who fails to see that there is a spiritual world that must be attended to with equal diligence.
- Everything he strives for in this life is lost forever—to be enjoyed by others but not him. The only thing he can keep in eternity is "treasure in heaven." And he has none.

- This way of life, which the world applauds, ends in death, and nothing.

5. **How can we can be infected by this way of thinking about our working lives. In what ways should we think differently to the world? What might it mean to be "rich toward God" in the way we think about work and retirement?**

- It's not about me! We can build our identity around work and reward; but that is missing the point of life.
- It is all about God. We must work trusting God for everything.
- Even our "retirement" must be thought about as a way of serving God and others—and not serving ourselves. Retirement is not a ceasing from work, but moving on to activity—"work"—that is continuing to contribute to the world, and to store up riches in heaven.
- The key point is that when we think that all this world is all that matters, and when we leave God out of the picture of our working lives, God's verdict is: "Fool."

6. **What other problems that flow from the fall can plague our working lives? Share with the group which of these you are most prone to, and discuss ways in which you can prevent yourself falling under their influence.**

Answers might include:

- *Meaninglessness:* (see Ecclesiastes 1). We can think, "What's the point of it all?" We need to remind ourselves that we are made for work, and through it we serve and bless others.
- *Anxiety:* (Look ahead to the next segment of Jesus' teaching in Luke 12). We can worry about all kinds of things related to work—our job security; our targets; what others think of us; what it provides for us, etc. We need to learn to trust the Lord in the details of our working lives. He is a worker, and the Giver of the creation command to work. We can trust him to look after us in it.
- *Conflict:* We should remind ourselves that conflict is inevitable in a fallen world, and often stems from greed and self centerdness (see James 3).
- *Workaholism:* We do not get our identity from work, but from Christ (see Ephesians 5:1-10).
- *Laziness:* We need to remember that we are working for Christ (see Ephesians 6:5-7).
- *Moral compromise:* We can sometimes be placed in situations where we are

pressured to compromise our Christian values. We must pray and seek wise counsel to determine if something is more of a cultural scruple, or is actually against the clear command of God to us in Scripture. We need to trust God as we resist ungodliness; and be prepared to resign if necessary (see Philippians 3:18-21).

Conflicting values: Sometimes things are not so black and white in our fallen world. While some issues call for Christian courage to stand up for what is right, others require deep discernment and wisdom to know how to deal with confusing problems. For example, a retail company that requires people to work on Sunday. Should the Christian worker or manager take their share of the Sunday work rota—and so bless and help others—or stand on a "sabbath" principle for themselves, that just rolls the burden onto others?

 READ LUKE 12:22-34

> **22 *Therefore I tell you, do not be anxious about your life, what you will eat, nor about your body, what you will put on.***

7. How does the Lord Jesus go on to reassure those who love him as they live in this fallen world?

- Trust God for your needs. Your heavenly Father knows what you need.
- Look at the evidence in creation of how the worker God cares for his world (v 24, 27)
- Seek God's kingdom first. God will supply all your needs.
- God is pleased to give us the kingdom (v 32). His grace is lavish and open-handed. We need to receive it.
- Consider where your treasure truly is (v 34). We need to think prayerfully and deeply about our motivations.
- Be generous.

8. Which of these encouragements do you most need to hear today and why?

Let the group share their particular needs relating to work, and then turn them into prayer. As a leader, be vigilant for signs of stress, overwork and potential burnout. Make a note to follow up with people during the week if there are any red flags that might indicate a more serious issue going on at work, home or in their spiritual lives.

Apply

FOR YOURSELF: Think about your own attitude toward work in our fallen world. Which of these might God call "foolish"? What does wisdom look like? Is there something that needs to be thought through? Who will you do that with? How terrible for God to think you a fool because you look for identity and meaning in the wrong place.

FOR YOUR CHURCH: Do you honor and encourage others at your church in their work? Are you supporting and helping each other as you deal with the issues and problems you face at work? Are you encouraging each other to work hard, but to value Christ more? If you are a church leader, when was the last time work was mentioned as part of the application in a sermon?

Pray

FOR YOUR GROUP: Pray for the issues that people raised in question 6. Ask God to give you courage and wisdom—and the discernment to know when to apply each!

FOR YOUR CHURCH: Ask the Lord to help you support each other as a church in your work struggles and dilemmas. And pray that you would encourage others to find their identity and meaning in Christ, not work.

FURTHER READING

Understanding this part of the Bible's story and work's place in it is actually crucial for us as Christians, because it helps explain why our work will always, to some degree or another, be marked by frustration. It shouldn't surprise us that work is difficult and painful sometimes.
Sebastian Traeger & Greg Gilbert

If you get mad at your Mac laptop and wonder who designed this demonic device, notice the manufacturer's icon on top: an apple with a bite out of it.
Peter Kreeft

Books

- *Every Good Endeavor*, part two (Timothy Keller with Katherine Leary Alsdorf)
- *Work Matters*, chapter two (Tom Nelson)
- *The Gospel at Work*, chapters one and two (Sebastian Traeger and Greg Gilbert)

Online

- *When Our Career Plans Aren't Panning Out*: gospelshapedchurch.org/resources421
- *Dear Graduates, A Glorious Commencement Awaits*: gospelshapedchurch.org/resources422
- *Lost Jobs, Found Church*: gospelshapedchurch.org/resources423

LEADER'S REFLECTIONS

SESSION 3:
RENEWED WORK

IT IS NOT ONLY PEOPLE THAT ARE BEING FREED FROM THE CONSEQUENCES OF SIN AND BROUGHT INTO FREEDOM AND THE PROMISE OF FUTURE RE-CREATION – IT IS THIS WORLD, TOO. AND THAT HAS PROFOUND CONSEQUENCES FOR HOW WE VIEW OUR WORK, IN ALL ITS UPS AND DOWNS.

TALK OUTLINE

3.1 • • We have seen that work can be hard and frustrating. But what if these difficulties are sent by God to make us more like Jesus?

- After Genesis 1 – 3 comes **redemption**. Redemption is *past* (at the cross), *present* (the ongoing work of God redeeming people today) and *future*—as we shall see in this session.

3.2 • **GOD IS RENEWING PEOPLE IN CHRIST** *Romans 8:18-23*

- God redeems fallen people by adopting us as his firstborn sons and heirs (v 23).
- Life is still marked by suffering and groaning (v 18), but we are destined for glory.
- Hardship in our work is part of the process that God uses to renew us into glory.
- **Work reshapes us**—either into the image of Christ, or into greater sin. We choose how we respond to hardship. *Give an example of how this might look in one line of work.*
- **Work refocuses our hope** (Romans 5:3-5). Because of the fall, we have placed our hope in the wrong things (like our career or relationships). But frustrations at work can help us refocus our hope on God.

3.3 • **GOD IS RENEWING CREATION**

- Creation is locked in a cycle of death and decay, but God is going to renew it so that it will flourish as he always intended it to (Romans 8:20-21).
- 2 Peter 3:10: Fire = purification. One day God will purify the earth from the curse, rather than destroy it altogether—a complete renewal and a radical healing.
- **Whatever you do, your work is done alongside God.** God is still working (Psalm 104:30). He works in and through us. *Give examples for different types of work.*
- **All good work has lasting value**—not just the work of pastors and missionaries! Any work that contributes towards greater honesty, joy and peace contributes toward this new creation. *Give examples.* Precisely how God will do this is a mystery, but this hope should infuse our work with new meaning.

• **CONCLUSION:** Romans 8 reminds us that we will suffer. But through our painful toil, God is both renewing us and his creation. One day we will see how he has taken our hard work and given it a lasting value we could never achieve ourselves.

You can download a full transcript of these talks at
WWW.GOSPELSHAPEDCHURCH.ORG/WORK/TALKS

RENEWED WORK

* Ask the group members to turn to Session 3 on page 51 of the Handbook.

▶ **WATCH DVD 3.1** (3 min 52 sec) **OR DELIVER TALK 3.1** (see page 70)

* Encourage the group to make notes as they watch the DVD or listen to the talk. There is space for notes on page 53 of the Handbook.

Discuss

👉 **READ ROMANS 8:18-23**

> [18] For I consider that the sufferings of this present time are not worth comparing with the glory that is to be revealed to us. [19] For the creation waits with eager longing for the revealing of the sons of God. [20] For the creation was subjected to futility, not willingly, but because of him who subjected it, in hope [21] that the creation itself will be set free from its bondage to corruption and obtain the freedom of the glory of the children of God. [22] For we know that the whole creation has been groaning together in the pains of childbirth until now. [23] And not only the creation, but we ourselves, who have the firstfruits of the Spirit, groan inwardly as we wait eagerly for adoption as sons, the redemption of our bodies.

What are God's people, Christians, waiting eagerly for? (v 23)

* "Adoption as sons"—being fully adopted by God into his family.
* "Redemption of our bodies"—to be redeemed means to be freed, released, bought back for a price.

NOTE: Romans 8:15 tells us that we "have received the Spirit of adoption as sons." This is the "firstfruits" Paul refers to in verse 23—we have already been legally adopted by God. But at the same time, we "eagerly await" becoming full members of God's family.

How are God's people described in verses 19, 21 and 23? Why do you think this is?

"Sons of God" (v 19), "children of God" (v 21), "sons" (v 23).

To be called sons or children of God shows the close family relationship God brings us into through Christ. This also makes Jesus our brother—something Paul picks up elsewhere in Romans 8 (eg: verse 17, where we are "fellow heirs with Christ", and verse 29, where Jesus is described as "the firstborn among many brothers").

But there is another reason why we should think of ourselves as a "son" of God (even if we are women). The reason Paul does not say we will become "sons and daughters" here is intentional, for he wants us to see that our inheritance is the same as that of the firstborn son in Paul's day. That is, everything that is the Father's will be ours. That is our inheritance. We who abandoned God will be adopted by that same God—and given the privileges of a firstborn son, because we are all in Christ, the firstborn over all creation.

What else will be redeemed and renewed (v 21-22)?

Creation itself will be redeemed (bought back, set free) from "its bondage to decay" (v21). This means the curse from Genesis 3 will be lifted.

▶ **WATCH DVD 3.2** (7 min 26 sec) **OR DELIVER TALK 3.2** (see page 70)

* *Encourage the group to make notes as they watch the DVD or listen to the talk. There is space for notes on page 54 of the Handbook.*

Discuss

"Work can either reshape us into the image of God or it can lead us into greater sin." Have you seen either or both of these things happening?

If people struggle to think of answers, start by reminding them of the example given by Tom in the DVD of someone working in a customer-service call center. That person can grow in their love for those they are serving, becoming more like Christ in the process—or they can become cynical, disrespectful and bitter toward those they are meant to be serving. Similarly, working in an unfair or hostile environment can help us grow in grace as we strive to be godly in our responses—or we can become angry and confrontational toward those we are working with.

READ ROMANS 5:3-5

> ³ Not only that, but we rejoice in our sufferings, knowing that suffering produces endurance, ⁴ and endurance produces character, and character produces hope, ⁵ and hope does not put us to shame, because God's love has been poured into our hearts through the Holy Spirit who has been given to us.

In the DVD, Tom said: "If we think suffering is bad and not from God, we will run away from it or grow bitter in it. But when we see it as coming from God's good hand, it can work in us to produce the priceless commodities of endurance, character and hope." How does this shape your view of work when it is difficult, exhausting or unfair?

Our immediate response to suffering can be to assume it is a bad thing, and so we do what we can to avoid it—and if we can't, we complain about it! But this passage in Romans 5 (and much of the rest of the Bible) sees suffering as being normal for Christians, something to "rejoice in", and that God will use to change us to be more like his Son. This change of viewpoint may be hard for some in your group to put into practice, even if they accept it in principle. It may help to make the idea more concrete if you ask questions such as: "What difference would this make to your thinking as you travel to work? How might it change your response when you feel you are being treated unfairly?"

How might God be using your workplace to produce an endurance in you? How might he be using it to refocus your hope on him?

Encourage group members to think of at least one example from their own daily occupation, reminding them that this doesn't have to mean paid employment. For example, how can a stay-at-home mom be growing in endurance as she cares for her toddler? How can someone who is unemployed grow in his hope in God as a result?

How did you respond to Tom's closing question: "Are you open to the possibility that God is seeking to use the frustrations and pain of your daily work to refocus our hopes around him?"

For some in the group this may be a new concept and/or one they really struggle to accept. You may simply want to encourage them to pray about this, asking God to work in their hearts so that they do become more open to the idea that he will bring suffering into their lives in order to refocus their hopes on him, and make them more like his Son.

WATCH DVD 3.3 (6 min 54 sec) **OR DELIVER TALK 3.3** (see page 70)

* *Encourage the group to make notes as they watch the DVD or listen to the talk. There is space for notes on page 56 of the Handbook.*

Discuss

Re-read Romans 8:19-22. As well as renewing people, God is in the business of renewing creation itself. How does Paul describe this process (v 22)? Why is this a good picture of what's happening to creation?

Romans 8:22 says: "The whole creation has been groaning together in the pains of childbirth". Childbirth can be very painful, and seem to last a very long time. In a similar way, creation is groaning now because it has been "subjected to futility" (v 20) and is in "bondage to decay" (v 21). However, at the end of childbirth comes the joy of new life—a joy that outweighs the pains leading up to it. Similarly, creation will be made new ("set free", v 21, though the exact way this will happen is a mystery to us).

In the DVD, Tom explained that we need to balance various passages in the Bible to get an understanding of what will happen to creation. In Revelation 21:1-5, everything is described as "new", but this doesn't need to mean the old has been completely destroyed. Instead, it is redeemed and renewed so that it is still recognizably the same, and yet completely perfected. A helpful illustration of this is Jesus' resurrection body. It was made new, with new abilities (such as being able to suddenly appear in locked rooms, John 20:26)—but in some ways it was still the old body, right down to the scars on his hands and side (John 20:27).

How will your own work (paid or otherwise) have lasting significance? How does your work create beauty, correct injustice, create peace, or lead to the flourishing of humanity?

These are hard things to understand, but it's not just creation that will be redeemed and renewed; so will our work. Tom explains: *"Whenever your work is in obedience to God, and you are in the service of others, you are not doing it alone, because God is at work in and through all you do."* All good work has lasting value, since God will one day renew this creation into one of beauty, justice, peace and truth.

Therefore, if group members can think of any example from their own work that "creates beauty, corrects injustice, creates peace, or leads to the flourishing of humanity", they can be encouraged for two reasons. They are serving God now and bringing glory to his name. And something of what they have done will also have lasting significance in God's refreshed creation.

Pray

Pray that God will remind you that "the sufferings of this present time are not worth comparing with the glory that is to be revealed to us" (Romans 8:18).

Ask God to enable to you to face the difficulties at work with faith, that they will reshape you into his image and refocus your hopes.

Thank God that one day the groaning, pain and futility of creation will be replaced by praise, healing and the restoration of his creation.

DAILY BIBLE DEVOTIONALS

These Bible devotionals work through Romans 1 – 3, taking us to the heart of why we need redemption, and how at the cross God provides that redemption. If you have group members about whose faith you are unsure, you might like to speak with them after these devotionals to find out how they have responded.

SERMONS

☞ **OPTION ONE: ROMANS 8:18-23**

This is the passage Tom looks at in his DVD presentation, which could be expanded upon in a sermon.

☞ **OPTION TWO: EXODUS 31:1-11**

This is the passage the Bible study is based on (see next page), which could also be expanded upon in a sermon.

☞ **OPTION THREE: JAMES 1:2-12**

- What we seek to feel: in our work and elsewhere, we can respond to trials with joy, because we know the Lord works in them to build our maturity (v 2-4).
- What we must ask for: wisdom, trusting that it will be given, and ensuring that we are committed to living by it (v 5-8).
- What we should remember: that the gospel lifts the lowly and humbles the rich—and that blessing lies in steadfastly loving God until eternity (v 9-12).

☞ **OPTION FOUR: GALATIANS 5:22 - PEACE AT WORK**

Church members will find a page to write notes on the sermon on page 69 of their Handbooks.

BIBLE STUDY

AIM: The main teaching session showed that not only will all God's people one day be redeemed (and should live this way now), but that all of God's creation will also be redeemed (and we should aim to contribute to that now). We can still create, cultivate and co-operate, and introduce glimpses of God's Eden perfection in this world. This Bible study in Exodus 31:1-11 takes us to Israel's time in the wilderness, and shows that God gives his people his Spirit in order that together they may do the work he calls them to do in order to build and extend the place of his presence—in this case, the tabernacle, but (as we will see) that tabernacle is a picture of Eden.

Discuss

When you think about the work of God's Holy Spirit in people, what do you think of him doing?

> Answers are likely to include some or all of enabling us to:
> - call on Jesus as our Lord (1 Corinthians 12:3)
> - fight our sin and grow godly fruit in us (Galatians 5:22-23)
> - recognize we are sinners and understand God is righteous (John 16:8-10)
> - use gifts that he gives to build up the church (1 Corinthians 12:4-11)
> - know how to defend ourselves when our faith brings us trouble (Matthew 10:19-20)

Additional question: What difference is there between the Spirit's work in the Old Testament and the New Testament?

> - In the Old Testament, the Spirit was given to only a few key people, for specific purposes (eg: Samson, King David), and he did not always remain for the whole lifetime of the believer. The difference between the Spirit's work in the Old Testament and in the New Testament is in scope and duration—the Spirit now dwells in all believers (Joel 2:28-29; Acts 2:1-4); and he dwells and works within us from the moment of our conversion (or even before), for the rest of our lives.

> It is unlikely that anyone will know about/remember the Spirit's indwelling of Bezalel and Oholiab, two Israelite craftsmen in the wilderness, to enable them

to do their work. If someone in your group thinks of them, then congratulate them—it is these two men whom this study is about!

READ EXODUS 31:1-11

> [6] I have called by name Bezalel the son of Uri, son of Hur, of the tribe of Judah and I have filled him with the Spirit of God, with ability and intelligence, with knowledge and all craftsmanship ... that they may make all that I have commanded you; the tent of meeting, and the ark of the testimony, and the mercy seat that is on it...

God speaks these words to Moses on the top of Mount Sinai, at the end of his instructions about how the Israelites are to build the "tent of meeting" (also called the "tabernacle")—the place where God will dwell among his people. The whole of chapters 25 – 30 have been taken up with detailed instructions given to Moses by the LORD as to how the tent of meeting is to be constructed.

1. Why is Bezalel so good at his job?

- Because God has filled him with the Spirit, who has given him his ability, intelligence, knowledge and craftsmanship (v 3).
- These Spirit-given gifts enable him to design, do metalwork (v 4), cut stones, carve wood, and more (v 5).

2. Why has God's Spirit given Bezalel, Oholiab and "all able men ability" (v 6-11)?

- So "that they may make all that I have commanded you: the tent of meeting" (v 7) and all that goes within it (v 7-11).
- God has given them these abilities so that they are able to make the tent of meeting "according to all that I have commanded [Moses]" (v 11). It is not only that these men will be able to build the tent of meeting, but that they will be able to build it exactly right, just as God wants it.

3. Look at the aspects of the tent of meeting that God picks out in v 7-11. What craftsman's skills will be required in order to do all this?

Tent-making; furnishings; woodwork; metalwork; perfume-making; tailoring.

4. The tent of meeting's design was intricate, inside and out. There was a reason for this. It was meant to point the Israelites somewhere else...

Complete the table:

TABERNACLE	EDEN
The materials used in the tent of meeting (25:3-7) The list begins with gold, and ends with onyx	**The materials found in Eden (Genesis 2:12)** Gold ... bdellium [aromatic resin] ... onyx
The lampstand that gives light to the tent of meeting looks like a tree (25:31-39); **The ark of the covenant in the center of the tent of meeting is where God meets Moses to** give his commands (ie: it is the place from which he rules) **(25:22)**	**In the center of Eden, there are two** trees **representing** the ability to live forever **and** God's rule (he is the one who "knows" ie: has authority over good and evil—humans do not/should not) (Genesis 2:9, 16-17)
The tabernacle instructions are structured around the phrase "The Lord said" **(25:1; 30:11, 17, 22, 34; 31:1, 12),** occuring seven **times**	**The creation is structured around the phrase** "God said" **(Gen 1:3, 6, 9, 14, 20, 24, 26), occuring** seven **times**
The instructions for building the tabernacle culminate with instructions about the Sabbath rest **(31:12-17)**	**The account of creation ends with a description of** the Sabbath rest **(Gen 2:1-3).**
Who is in the tent of meeting? (25:8) God—it is his "sanctuary", where he will "dwell among" his people. So the tent of meeting is where God meets humanity.	**Who is in the Garden of Eden (2:21-22; 3:8)?** God, and people. In Eden, God and humanity dwelled together—God "walked" among his people (until the fall shattered this paradise)

5. What is the tent of meeting meant to remind the Israelites of?

The Garden of Eden. It is a signpost back to the perfect place of God's presence (and therefore forwards, too, to the new creation, when God will restore his world and live with his people—see Revelation 21:1-4)

6. What were Adam and Eve put in Eden to do (Genesis 1:28; 2:15, 18)?

To work it and look after it; and, by implication from 1:28, to extend it, so that Eden covered the face of the earth. (2:10-14 gives the sense of the rivers of the earth having their source in Eden—the idea being that as the water spreads from Eden to irrigate the earth, so humans are to spread from Eden to cultivate the earth). So the humans were to keep Eden, and extend Eden.

7. How are Bezalel and Oholiab engaged in the same kind of work?

They are, in co-operation with each other, to use their work skills to build the "Eden" place of the Tent of Meeting. And they have the presence of God with them to do this, by his Spirit.

8. How can we be engaged in the same kind of work?

Anytime we seek to use our work skills and vocational situations to extend the realities of Eden into a new place or in a new way, we are doing what Adam and Eve did, and what Bezalel and Oholiab did. And God's Spirit dwells in us to enable this. We do not have vocational giftings by accident, nor simply for our own sake, but to enable this world to be more like, and to point to, Eden.

Apply

FOR YOURSELF: What abilities and passions has the Spirit given you that you use in the workplace? How can you be engaged in extending Eden, with God's help and in co-operation with others? How does this both excite you about your work, and challenge you in the way you view and go about your work?

FOR YOUR CHURCH: How often do you encourage each other (both during the service and in your conversations afterwards) to have this view of your Monday-Friday lives? How will you, as a group, proactively pursue the promotion of this kind of view of your vocations?

Pray

FOR YOUR GROUP: Thank God that he cares about, empowers, and uses your work when it is done under his rule, for his glory. Share how you find it hard to see your work in this way, and pray for one another.

FOR YOUR CHURCH: Pray that you would be a community that challenges one another to see work as a way to be part of God's purposes for his world; and a church that equips you for your weekly work, whether in the home, the field, the factory or the office, as well as for your Sunday worship.

FURTHER READING

No more let sin or sorrows grow,
Nor thorns infest the ground;
He comes to make his blessings flow
Far as the curse is found.
Isaac Watts

Difficulties, disappointments, discouragements, and suffering are a part
of every work experience, but they need not be seen as obstacles to God's
purposes in our lives.
Tom Nelson

Work saves us from three great evils: boredom, vice and greed.
Voltaire

Books

- *Romans 8 – 16 For You, chapter three (Timothy Keller)*
- *Eternity Changes Everything (Stephen Witmer)*
- *The Gospel at Work, chapter four (Sebastian Traeger and Greg Gilbert)*
- *Gospel-Centered Work (Tim Chester)*
- *Explicit Gospel (Matt Chandler)*

Online

- *Rethinking Heaven: gospelshapedchurch.org/resources431*
- *Say Goodbye to Lifeboat Theology: gospelshapedchurch.org/resources432*
- *When Faith Meets Work (video):*
  gospelshapedchurch.org/resources433

LEADER'S REFLECTIONS

SESSION 4:

GLORIFYING GOD THROUGH WORK

HAVE YOU EVER SEEN YOUR WORKPLACE AS A GREAT PLACE FOR YOUR OWN DISCIPLESHIP – A PLACE WHERE YOU CAN REALLY GROW AND SERVE? IN THIS SESSION, WE'LL CONNECT OUR COMMITMENT TO FOLLOWING CHRIST WITH OUR LIVES FROM MONDAY TO FRIDAY.

TALK OUTLINE

4.1 • Most of us have a tendency toward dualism—putting our work life and spiritual life in two separate boxes. This is wrong, because:
- it suggests that secular work cannot please Christ.
- we are to work in light of who we are as Christians.

4.2 • **WHOLE-LIFE DISCIPLESHIP** *Matthew 11:28-30*
Jesus calls us to *whole-life* discipleship. He invites us to take his yoke, follow his lead and learn from him. There are three crucial ideas…

• **A YOKE FOR ALL OF LIFE**
Following Jesus is for all of life. When people encounter Jesus, he affects their work (for example, Zacchaeus, Luke 19:1-10). He doesn't necessarily call us to change jobs, but he challenges how we do them.

• **A YOKE THAT IS CUSTOM-MADE**
Your work situation is custom-made to lead you to maturity. This could be to:
- **love your neighbor**—your co-workers and the people you serve
- **do and love justice**—through relief or reform
- **share the gospel**—by living and speaking distinctively through work's ups and downs
- **do good work well** and help people flourish (Colossians 3:23-24)
- **create beauty** and point to the Creator God
- **worship God** through your work
- **enable generosity**—with your free time, technical skills or money

4.3 • **A YOKE THAT OFFERS REST**
- **The rest of Jesus refreshes**—when work is hard, we can rest in Christ's finished work, knowing that our frustrations will not have the last word.
- **Jesus cures our restlessness**—the gospel frees us from our addiction to working ourselves to the bone in order to make a name for ourselves, because we know that the Name above all names has already given himself for us.

• **CONCLUSION:** *Re-read Matthew 11:28-30.* What could be better than this?!

You can download a full transcript of these talks at
WWW.GOSPELSHAPEDCHURCH.ORG/WORK/TALKS

GLORIFYING GOD THROUGH WORK

* *Ask the group members to turn to Session 4 on page 71 of the Handbook.*

WATCH DVD 4.1 (3 min 52 sec) **OR DELIVER TALK 4.1** (see page 88)

* *Encourage the group to make notes as they watch the DVD or listen to the talk. There is space for notes on page 73 of the Handbook.*

Discuss

How did you react to Tom's "confession" of having failed his church?

The way people answer this question will give a feel for how serious they think it is to separate our view of work from our view of parts of life that may seem more obviously "Christian." This is an issue that will be addressed during this session.

Which of these errors are you more likely to fall into?

* **Thinking you can only please God through your work if it directly promotes the gospel.**
* **Thinking of yourself as a Christian only when involved in church activity.**

If we have a wrong view of work, we can split our life into two separate areas that are not related to each other—one spiritual and the other physical; one sacred and the other secular. This is called "dualism."

As we will see in the next DVD section, the Bible doesn't divide life in this way. The gospel doesn't just apply to Sunday services and activity that is explicitly Christian—it speaks into the whole of our lives.

▶ **WATCH DVD 4.2** (11 min 15 sec) **OR DELIVER TALK 4.2** (see page 88)

* *Encourage the group to make notes as they watch the DVD or listen to the talk. There is space for notes on page 74 of the Handbook.*

Discuss

 **READ MATTHEW 11:28-30**

> Jesus said:
> ²⁸ *Come to me, all who labor and are heavy laden, and I will give you rest.*
> ²⁹ *Take my yoke upon you, and learn from me, for I am gentle and lowly in heart, and you will find rest for your souls.* ³⁰ *For my yoke is easy, and my burden is light.*

As you think of Jesus' image of a yoke, what do you find most encouraging? What is most challenging?

> If needed, remind the group how a yoke works: a farmer puts a mature, experienced ox on one side and the younger, inexperienced ox on the other. The mature ox keeps the young ox on course, but they work together in harness to get the job done. Jesus' example of a yoke is encouraging because his "yoke is easy" and his "burden is light." He is "gentle" as we "learn from him", and we will "find rest for our souls." The picture of a yoke is challenging because as we "learn from Jesus," he will keep us going the way he wants, which may be new, scary or simply a direction in which we don't naturally want to go!

1. A YOKE FOR ALL OF LIFE

If Jesus' yoke is for all of life, that means *everything* we do, including our daily occupation, paid or otherwise. "*Jesus does not necessarily call us to change our job, but he does challenge us about how we do our job.*" How have you been challenged so far while working through this curriculum?

> This is an opportunity to recap some of the things you've been discussing so far in this curriculum. It will also give you a feel for where each group member is at in their thinking about work.

2. A CUSTOM-MADE YOKE

"Your work situation is a custom-made yoke for you. Jesus is using the unique way you are wired and gifted, along with the work situation you find yourself in, to provoke and lead you to maturity." Think about the seven areas we looked at:

- To love your neighbor
- To love justice
- To share the gospel
- To do good work, well done
- To create beauty
- To worship God
- To enable generosity

Which of these primarily apply to how you serve God in your own work situation? How have you seen this play out in your work?

As was made clear in the DVD, most people will find that only some of these seven areas apply within their own work situation. Encourage everyone in your group to mention at least one of the seven areas, and to say how they have seen this play out in their own workplace.

In the DVD presentation, Tom described the workplace as being like a classroom, where God is teaching us, and where we can learn and practice. In which of these areas do you feel you have the most need to learn and practice? What are some practical ways in which you can grow in these areas?

Encourage group members to be both honest about the areas they need to grow in, and practical about how that might happen. For example, thinking how their work situation can help them to love their neighbor more, who in particular they need to be more loving, forgiving or generous towards, and how might they do or be that this week? Similarly, if they want to grow in sharing the gospel, when is a good time to chat with colleagues, and is there anything current in the news or popular culture that could be a starting point for discussing a biblical viewpoint this week?

You must also note that *growing often involves failure*, and learning from our mistakes. This is an opportunity for Christians to model genuine confession—owning up to mistakes; and genuine repentance—showing real sorrow for the problems or hurt we have caused colleagues of customers, and working at changing as a result. This attitude is uncommon in many workplaces, where people want to pass the blame to others, and are resistant to change. But Christians can be a genuine witness for their faith if they practice this, as well as being a force for good in their work.

▶ **WATCH DVD 4.3** (2 min 42 sec) **OR DELIVER TALK 4.3** (see page 88)

* *Encourage the group to make notes as they watch the DVD or listen to the talk. There is space for notes on page 77 of the Handbook.*

Discuss

3. A YOKE THAT OFFERS REST

Why is it liberating to tie our identity to Christ and not to our work?

Whatever our work situation, whether frustrating or encouraging, it is liable to change, sometimes with no warning. But a Christian's identity in Christ doesn't change. No amount of work can ever earn us the status we have as children of God, adopted into his family and fully forgiven for all our sins. And neither can any "failure" in our work make God love us any less. Even if our previous co-workers turn against us, and our work is taken away from us, God will not reject us or send us out of his family. Our identity in Christ is certain and secure.

If your work is frustrating, why is the "rest" of Jesus such good news?

As Tom says in the DVD presentation: *"The 'rest' of Jesus means we can rest in his finished work. He has defeated death, sin and evil, which does not just mean our sins will be forgiven if we are in Christ. It also means that Jesus will one day undo all the injustice and toil in work and in the whole of life. We can rest in his finished work, knowing our trials and frustrations will not have the last word."*

If you love your job or are successful in your work, what does the "rest" of Jesus help you remember?

It is perhaps particularly easy for someone who is successful in work to tie their identity to their work. When work is going well, we feel great; but when it isn't, we don't. Or we may find ourselves working longer and longer hours in order to continue to be as successful as possible. (For those who are married or with children, this can lead to neglecting our families. For those who are single, it's easy to convince ourselves that this level of work is fine because it's not affecting anyone other than ourselves.) The "rest" of Jesus reminds us not to put too high a value on the success or otherwise of our work. Our status in Christ is the only one that will last into eternity—and it is certain and secure because his work is finished.

In both cases, what difference will this make in the coming week?

Encourage group members to give practical answers to this question—how will their viewpoints and actions reflect the fact that their eternal rest lies in the finished work of Christ? When will they most need to remember and live out the truth that they have "rest" in and with Jesus?

Pray

"Come to me, all who labor and are heavy laden, and I will give you rest. Take my yoke upon you, and learn from me, for I am gentle and lowly in heart, and you will find rest for your souls. For my yoke is easy, and my burden is light."

Pray through each line of Jesus' words in turn, thanking him for his promise of rest, and asking him to help you learn from him as you "take his yoke upon you."

DAILY BIBLE DEVOTIONALS

Encourage your group members at the end of the main teaching session to keep studying, or start to study, the daily devotionals. This week they are focused on how we can live and speak as effective witnesses to Christ in our workplaces (factory, field, office or home), studying Paul's words in Colossians 4:2-6.

SERMONS

OPTION ONE: MATTHEW 11:28-30

This is the passage Tom bases his teaching on in his DVD presentation, which could be expanded upon in a sermon.

OPTION TWO: COLOSSIANS 3:1-17

This is the passage the Bible study is based on (see next page), which could also be expanded upon in a sermon.

OPTION THREE: LUKE 3:1-17

- John the Baptist urgently called people to repent—and real repentance means real changes, or "fruit," in our lives (v 7-9).
- John called people not to change their trade, but to conduct themselves within their trade differently—generously and honestly (v 10-14).
- John pointed to a mightier One, who would bring the Spirit to enable repentant living, and would also bring judgment to the world (v 15-17).

OPTION FOUR: GALATIANS 5:22 - PATIENCE AT WORK

Church members will find a page to write notes on the sermon on page 89 of their Handbooks.

BIBLE STUDY

AIM: The main teaching session this week encouraged us to think about the discipleship that Jesus calls us to: it's for the *whole of life*—including our work. This Bible study grapples with some of the big changes in attitude and lifestyle that our belonging to Christ brings with it.

Discuss

If you were to ask a random group of people in the street what they think of Christians and churches, what are some of the answers you think they might give? Do you think their assessment would be fair?

Typical answers to this might be that they think Christians are hypocrites, judgmental, homophobic, morally self-righteous, etc. Intriguingly, however, most surveys suggest that those who think Christians are like this are relatively few (if rather more vociferous than others about their criticisms). Most people who know genuine believers know them to be kind, friendly, concerned, helpful and loving.

READ COLOSSIANS 3:1-17

> *7 In these you too once walked, when you were living in them. 8 But now you must put them all away: anger, wrath, malice, slander, and obscene talk from your mouth.*

1. **What has already happened to Christians, according to Paul in v 1-3? What do you think these statements mean?**

   - We have died with Christ (v 3). We have been forgiven through the death of Jesus, and our old life is now at an end.
   - We have been raised with Christ (v 1). We have been given new life through Jesus' resurrection.
   - Our true life is now "hidden with Christ." Our salvation is secure. We are not outwardly what we truly are as people who belong to Christ.

What will happen in the future (v 4)?

When Christ returns, our real life will be revealed along with him. The world will see what believers are really like in their inner selves—washed clean by Jesus: made holy and righteous because of his work for us.

2. **What does Paul say should drive our thinking about life now?**

   - Because we have died with Christ, we should view our old way of life as something past.
   - Because we have been raised with Christ, and our future is secure, we should raise our sights and see everything from the perspective of eternity.
   - This means focusing our minds on the things that last into eternity—including every good work that we do (see Session 3).

3. **Some people accuse Christians of being "so heavenly minded that they are of no earthly use." How would you reply to that accusation from this passage?**

   - Setting our minds on "the things that are above" should make us more useful and practical. Focusing on eternal values (v 1-4) leads to extremely practical changes in our behavior now (v 5-11)
   - It is true that there might be some Christians who have a world-denying spirituality but they have fallen into the trap of thinking, falsely, that our life and work in the here and now is of little importance in the face of eternity.
   - Rightly understood, verses 1-4 will drive believers to apply the gospel to their everyday lives, which will lead them to be more engaged with the world and practical in the way they live.

4. **What does an understanding of our new life in Christ lead us to do (v 5)? Which of the qualities in verses 5 and 8 do you struggle most to leave behind, especially in the course of your daily occupation?**

   - We will "put to death" the way we used to live. And we will "put on" the new life. Notice the four pictures Paul uses here: "put to death" (kill!); "once walked" (pathway/direction); "put ... away" (like throwing out the garbage); "put off" (removing an old set of filthy clothes).
   - Group members may talk about the different ways that the things listed in these verses are displayed in the office.

- Particular struggles will be different for different people, eg: a parent with small children may struggle with anger; another person may find it hard not to join in with unhelpful office banter; someone else may find it hard not to be covetous because of the motivation of money at the heart of many jobs.
- We should not give in an ostentatious way, but quietly, secretly and humbly—not looking for approval from anyone but the Lord (Matthew 6:1-4).

5. What further encouragements are there to work at growing in our holiness (v 6, 12) How will we grow in our godliness (v 10, 16)?

- **The coming judgment of God (v 6):** Through Jesus' death we have been rescued from the wrath that is to come, which we deserved for living like this. Why would we indulge these things in our daily lives now, particularly when we know that these things are hated by our Father who loves us, and are the things for which Christ died?
- **We have been chosen (v 12):** What a privilege to be called by Jesus to belong to him. We will not want to abuse our privilege and be ungrateful.
- **We grow through understanding God's word (v 16):** As we allow the word of Christ to dwell in us richly. Practically, this will mean that we listen to sermons and attend Bible studies, where we have the opportunity teach, encourage, and admonish one another. But more, it means that we will meditate on the Bible's teaching and allow it to change us—God's word will "dwell in [us] richly"—not in a shallow or superficial way.
- **Worship (v 16):** Singing is a way in which Christians allow the truth of the gospel to permeate their minds, hearts and emotions. We should not underestimate the power that praise and thanksgiving have to change our lives as we worship together.

6. How will the qualities of your renewed life (v 11-14) be distinctive in the place where you work?

- Paul writes primarily about our lives together as Christians, but these attitudes will flow over into our workplaces.
- The answers will be different, but we will want to talk about racism and sexism (v 11), uncaring attitudes, abuse of power, gratitude and forgiveness.
- Believers should also be quick to own up to mistakes and failure in the workplace—modeling genuine regret and being willing to repent of bad attitudes or practices and change. Likewise, we should not hold grudges against fellow workers or customers who have wronged us in some way.

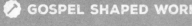

- Take time to ask the question: *How can you model and encourage these Christian qualities in your workplace, without being perceived as a spoilsport or busybody?* However, you should be clear that being distinctively Christian may inevitably lead to persecution in your workplace.

7. How might your workplace be more enjoyable, and more productive and efficient, if it displayed the qualities in verses 12-13?

Try to help people see that this is not just about "niceness," but that workplaces waste a huge amount of time and effort through bad relationships. Gratitude and thankfulness can improve the way people work and enjoy work enormously.

8. What does it mean to do "everything in the name of the Lord Jesus"? What will verse 17 mean in practice for you in the workplace?

- If you are a Christian, then you are Christ's person. You were chosen by him; you belong to him; you are kept safe by him; you will be revealed with him in glory; he is your Lord and Savior. This means that everything we do must be brought under his lordship, and be done for his honor—including every aspect of our working lives.
- All our actions, conversations and relationships at work come under this heading! There is no part of your life that you can keep for yourself, to do with as you want.
- It does not mean that you will shout out: "in Jesus' name" at regular intervals at work. In fact, you should not need to, because you will work in a way that honors him. And you will give thanks to God for your work when things go wrong and when things go right.

Apply

FOR YOURSELF: What one quality can you work on growing in your life this week that will be especially beneficial to you and your colleagues at work?

FOR YOUR CHURCH: How can you encourage the peace of Christ to rule among you? How can you encourage the word of Christ to dwell more richly among you? What does "teaching and admonishing one another" look like in your congregational life? How can you encourage a communal sense of gratitude toward God to characterize your lives, rather than grumbling, discord and discontent?

Pray

FOR YOUR GROUP: Pray for your specific answers in question 4. Ask the Lord to help you recognize how and when you are tempted to live this way, and to bring to mind our privilege and status as chosen children. Spend some time giving thanks for your work—both the great things, and the things you find difficult and struggle with.

FOR YOUR CHURCH: Pray that the qualities of our renewed life would be evident in your whole church, and that you would each continue to grow as the word of Christ dwells richly among you.

FURTHER READING

Calling is the truth that God calls us to himself so decisively that everything we are, everything we do, and everything we have is invested with a special devotion and dynamism lived out as a response to his summons and service.
Os Guinness

It is often hard to get Christians to see that God is willing not just to use men and women in ministry, but in law, in medicine, in business, in the arts. This is the great shortfall today.
Dick Lucas

Living out my faith in my work seemed relegated to small symbolic gestures, to self-righteous abstinence from certain behaviors, and to political alignments on the top cultural and legal issues of the day.
Katherine Leary Alsdorf

Books

- *The Call (Os Guinness)*
- *God at Work, chapters ten to eleven (Gene Veith)*
- *Gospel Centered Discipleship (Jonathan Dodson)*
- *Discipleship Matters (Peter Maiden)*
- *Questioning Evangelism (Randy Newman)*

Online

- Don't Track Your Success: gospelshapedchurch.org/resources441
- Your Job is God's Assignment: gospelshapedchurch.org/resources442
- Workplace Culture: Pain, Possiblity and Empowerment (video): gospelshapedchurch.org/resources443
- Lay Aside the Weight of Restless Work: gospelshapedchurch.org/resources444
- 100,000 Hours: Eight Aims for your Career: gospelshapedchurch.org/resources445

LEADER'S REFLECTIONS

SESSION 5:

THE GOSPEL
AND YOUR WORK

ALL OF US HAVE A "STORY" THROUGH WHICH WE SEE THE WORLD, OUR LIVES, AND OUR WORK. THAT STORY, FOR EACH OF GOD'S PEOPLE, NEEDS TO BE THE GOSPEL. BUT WHAT WILL THAT LOOK LIKE FOR OUR APPROACH TO OUR OCCUPATION? HOW MIGHT THAT SHAPE OUR VIEW OF OTHERS? AND WHAT CAN A RELATIONSHIP BETWEEN A MASTER AND HIS SLAVE IN THE FIRST CENTURY TEACH US ABOUT OUR LIVES IN THE TWENTY-FIRST?

TALK OUTLINE

5.1 • What does it mean to be a Christian and a… *[insert job here]*? How do we connect Sunday to Monday? God wants us to view our work as part of the gospel story. We're looking at Philemon, and the context is one of slavery. In Philemon, Paul does not strongly rebuke slavery, probably because slavery at this time was not like chattel slavery in early-modern US and Europe; and Paul speaks against it in more subtle ways. His letter is about two Christians—Onesimus, a slave, and Philemon, his master.

5.2 • **TWO STORIES**
The gospel gave both Philemon and Onesimus a new story through which to view their work. Paul challenges Philemon to shine the gospel on his work.

• **CHANGE HOW YOU SEE OTHERS**
As a slave, Onesimus was "useless" (v 11). But now the gospel has transformed his attitude so that he is "useful"—Paul's "very heart." Philemon needs to see slaves through the gospel story—as human beings with the potential to serve God well.

• **CHANGE THE WAY YOU SEE WORK**
• Philemon is an overseer not just to advance himself, but with the responsibility to see the flourishing of all those in his care.
• Onesimus was transformed under Paul's leadership. The implicit question is: *Why didn't that happen under Philemon's care?*
• Verse 19: No debt will ever mirror the debt Christ has paid on the cross. The gospel is valuable! And it should now inform how Philemon thinks of his slaves.

5.3 • **CONCLUSION**
This is the gospel story that we are in:
• **The world is good** (Genesis 1)—so work is inherently good.
• **The world is fallen** (Genesis 3)—so work is now hard and frustrating.
• **The gospel is at work**—Jesus died and rose again and is calling to himself a new community. His disciples are different to the world.
• **The world will be redeemed** (Romans 8)—both physical creation and humans.
In light of this, Christians will view their work differently than the world does.

You can download a full transcript of these talks at
WWW.GOSPELSHAPEDCHURCH.ORG/WORK/TALKS

THE GOSPEL AND YOUR WORK

▶ **WATCH DVD 5.1** (3 min 51 sec) **OR DELIVER TALK 5.1** (see page 106)

* *Encourage the group to make notes as they watch the DVD or listen to the talk. There is space for notes on page 93 of the Handbook.*

👉 *Discuss*

PHILEMON V 10-17

> ¹⁰ *I appeal to you for my child, Onesimus, whose father I became in my imprisonment.* ¹¹ *(Formerly he was useless to you, but now he is indeed useful to you and to me.)* ¹² *I am sending him back to you, sending my very heart.* ¹³ *I would have been glad to keep him with me, in order that he might serve me on your behalf during my imprisonment for the gospel,* ¹⁴ *but I preferred to do nothing without your consent in order that your goodness might not be by compulsion but of your own accord.* ¹⁵ *For this perhaps is why he was parted from you for a while, that you might have him back forever,* ¹⁶ *no longer as a bondservant but more than a bondservant, as a beloved brother—especially to me, but how much more to you, both in the flesh and in the Lord.*
> ¹⁷ *So if you consider me your partner, receive him as you would receive me.*

How does Paul refer to the slave Onesimus? What does Paul think of him?

Paul refers to Onesimus as "my child" (v 10), "useful" (v 11), "my very heart" (v 12), and "beloved brother" (v 16). Paul loves Onesimus dearly, and says he "would have been glad to keep him with me" (v 13).

What appeal does Paul make to Philemon?

Paul wants Philemon to welcome his former slave back, but "no longer as a bondservant" (v 16). Instead, Paul appeals to Philemon to welcome Onesimus back as a "beloved brother." ("Bondservant" is a translation of the Greek word *doulos*, which means "one who is subservient to, and entirely at the disposal of, his master". It can also be translated as "slave.")

Why might Philemon find it difficult to accept Onesimus "as a beloved brother"?

Both men are used to being in a master-slave relationship, rather than relating to one another as brothers. Also, although we don't know the details, their previous relationship was clearly a difficult one, with Philemon believing that Onesimus was "useless to him" (v 11). In the eyes of Roman law, the fault would all be with the slave, so Paul is asking Philemon, a Roman citizen, to view his former slave very differently than he was used to.

▶ **WATCH DVD 5.2** (11 min 15 sec) **OR DELIVER TALK 5.2** (see page 106)

* *Encourage the group to make notes as they watch the DVD or listen to the talk. There is space for notes on page 94 of the Handbook.*

Discuss

What stories does our culture tell us about being employed, and being an employer?

Your "stories" will vary according to the culture you are in. However, a number of the following may apply:

- "Our value is closely tied with our employment, with the highest value given to those with high-profile and/or highly-paid jobs, and the lowest value to those doing dirty, manual labor or who are unemployed."
- "Going out to work is more valuable than staying at home bringing up children."
- "Work is *more* important than church, family or leisure."
- "Work is *less* important than church, family or leisure."
- "We need to earn as much as possible now so that we can enjoy the good life when we retire."
- "If I'm an employer, I am more important than my employees."
- "I have the right to make my employees stay late and work extra hours whenever I choose. If they don't like it, they can go and get another job."

How does the gospel message challenge those stories, both for employer and employee?

- As we saw in Session 4, if we are Christians, then our identity is found in Christ, not in whatever job we do or don't have.
- As we saw in Session 3, all work done in obedience to God, and that contributes to the flourishing of others, is of eternal value. This includes bringing up children, or staying at home to look after those who are elderly or unwell.
- If we view life through the gospel story, we see that every part of life is affected by the gospel. So rather than thinking of work as either *more* or *less* important than the other parts of our life, everything we do should be in service to God and to bring honor to his name.
- We have something far better than retirement to look forward to! Because of Christ, we can look forward to being with him in the new creation. In the meantime, retirement may give us more time and flexibility to serve God in our local church, or even to be involved with mission elsewhere.
- As we have seen in the book of Philemon, the gospel story changes how we view people. The fact that someone is our employee does not make them of less importance—and if that person is a Christian, then they are a "beloved brother" or sister.
- In Session 1, we saw that we are made in God's image. If we are going to reflect God's goodness and justice in our own lives, we will treat our employees fairly.

Which story do you tell yourself most often during a working week? What effect does this have on you?

Encourage every group member to give an answer to these questions, so that they can see how their "story" shapes the way they do their work, react to setbacks, treat others, and so on. Some may give a "story" that has already been discussed—others may have a different story to talk about.

▶ **WATCH DVD 5.3** (2 min 37 sec) **OR DELIVER TALK 5.3** (see page 106)

* *Encourage the group to make notes as they watch the DVD or listen to the talk. There is space for notes on page 96 of the Handbook.*

Discuss

What do you think is the difference between someone who calls themselves "a Christian plumber" and someone who would describe themselves as "a plumber who is also a Christian"?

A "Christian plumber" will view everything they do, including all their plumbing work, through the gospel story. They want to serve and honor God in the quality, efficiency and care of their work. They will want to show God's loving care in their relationships with co-workers and customers, and to show God's creative care in the way they do their practical tasks.

The alternative is subtle, but profound. Someone who sees themselves primarily as a plumber, who is also a Christian, has, in effect, put the two activities in separate boxes. Their Christian life is separate from their working activities.

Imagine holding up a sign like the ones at the start of the DVD. It says: "I am a _____" (fill in your own daily occupation). Now put the word "Christian" in front of your occupation. Is this how you usually see yourself? What difference would it / does it make to how you view your daily occupation?

Encourage every member of the group to think about this, whatever their daily occupation might be, paid or otherwise. Challenge them to think about how the gospel story makes a difference to how they view their own work, in a similar way to how Paul challenged Philemon to view his role as an overseer differently (and therefore view Onesimus differently too).

How do the people you work with see you? As a _____ who also happens to be a Christian? Or do they see you as a Christian _____? And if it's the first, what changes might you make so that they come to see you as the second instead?

Talk about some practical things you can do that will make it more obvious to your co-workers that you are a Christian, and that you view your work accordingly. This might include how you do your job, how you treat your colleagues, what you do during lunch breaks, how you talk about your weekends, etc. Encourage your group to come up with two or three specific changes they can make in the next month—and make sure you follow up with them in a month's time.

Pray

Has the letter to Philemon challenged the way in which you are viewing your own daily occupation? Talk to God about your answers.

Thank God for the gospel story—creation, fall, redemption and new creation. Thank him that you are part of that story because of Jesus.

Ask God to help you to view the whole of your life, including work, through the gospel story.

DAILY BIBLE DEVOTIONALS

The main session encouraged us to consider how the gospel must change the way we view our workplaces, and live within our work contexts. So these devotionals work through 1 Peter 2:11-25, where the apostle exhorts Christians to live in a way that is "honorable" and causes others to glorify God, and shows how Christ's example defines and inspires honorable conduct when under pressure.

SERMONS

OPTION ONE: PHILEMON

This is the epistle from which Tom draws his insights in his DVD presentation, and (since it is a short epistle) it could also be expanded upon in a sermon.

OPTION TWO: COLOSSIANS 3:22 – 4:1

Following from the Bible study in the previous session, the Bible study is based on this passage (see next page), which could also be preached on.

OPTION THREE: EPHESIANS 6:5-9

- First-century Christian bondservants and twenty-first-century Christian workers are to do all their work in the sight of Christ (v 5).
- Knowing we are working for Christ means we are freed from seeking to impress others (v 6-7)—we seek the reward of the Lord's approval, not man's (v 8).
- First-century Christian masters and twenty-first-century Christian bosses, line managers etc., must treat those in their care as their divine Master treats them.

OPTION FOUR: GALATIANS 5:22 – KINDNESS & GOODNESS AT WORK

Church members will find a page to write notes on the sermon on page 109 of their Handbooks.

BIBLE STUDY

AIM: This week's main teaching session has focused on how belonging to Christ transforms both our view of the world—cutting through the accepted cultural values of the day—and, in particular, our attitude toward working relationships. In this study, we will look at a Bible passage that gives more detail on how Christ transforms our view of work.

Discuss

What different motivations do people have to work? Can you think of examples of people you know who are driven by each of these? What motivations have you had in some of the work you have done in the past?

This is meant to be a fun question to get people into thinking about motivation. Some answers might include: money; desperation; the fun of working with a particular group of people; believing in the product or mission of the organization; career advancement, etc. Encourage the group to share stories, both positive and negative, about people motivated by these things, eg: a colleague who would do anything to advance in their career, or someone who worked incredibly hard in a charity because they were passionate about the problem they were trying to solve.

In this Bible study, we are going to look at Paul's instructions to slaves and masters in the letter to the Colossians—sent at the same time as the letter to Philemon. Are you prepared to be challenged about your own attitude toward work?

READ COLOSSIANS 3:22-4:6

23 Whatever you do, work heartily, as for the Lord and not for men, 24 knowing that from the Lord you will receive the inheritance as your reward. You are serving the Lord Christ.

NOTE: In the first part of chapter 3, the Colossians have been reminded that being a Christian is a massive privilege. We have been chosen by Christ; we have died with Christ; we have been raised with him and kept safe by him; and who we truly are will be revealed on the last day. The gospel qualities of peace and gratitude should suffuse our lives, and particularly our lives in fellowship with one another, as we allow the word of Christ to dwell in us richly.

1. **What qualities should bondservants or slaves bring to their obedience to earthly masters?**

   - Completeness: they are to obey "in everything."
   - Integrity: ie: not as "eye-pleasers"—people who only work when the boss is watching. They must be hard workers whoever is watching.
   - Sincerity: we must not put on an act at work, but find ways in which we can honorably be enthusiastic about work.
   - Humility: we measure ourselves against the Lord—not our masters or fellow workers. We are to be humble before others as well as before God.

2. **Why might these commands still be relevant, but hard to follow in your working situation?**

   - Human nature has not changed! We are all still prone to laziness, people-pleasing and "putting on an act" in our work.
   - We might be working in a company we do not believe in, or for a boss who demands difficult or pointless things from us. There may be a culture of "doing the minimum" in your workplace that is hard to push against. There may be systems in place that mean you are misunderstood when you try harder or better, because they are constructed for people whose default is to avoid any hard work.

3. **What should motivate Christians to be different?**

   - "Fearing the Lord" v 22: Note that "fear" can include positive as well as negative aspects like respect for someone's authority. Some managers and companies may use fear as a motivator—you will lose your job, be disciplined, or fail to advance in your career. Christians will be motivated by their love and respect for God, who is Lord of their lives. We will not fear what earthly masters may do to us, but we fear the disapproval of our Lord, and we will love to be obedient to his commands.

- "Receive … [a] reward" v 24: Many people work for the earthly rewards of money, respect from others, power or self approval. Christians will see all these things through the lens of the greater inheritance we will receive in eternity with Christ.

4. What help is there here for a slave who is working for a bad master? How will this help you when you are treated unfairly at work?

- v 25: God will judge all of us. However badly we are treated, we know that God will bring all injustices to book one day. No one will ever "get away with it."
- Our natural reaction when treated badly is to accuse, complain, murmur, grumble, judge, seek revenge, etc. Christians can be wonderfully free from these responses as we entrust ourselves to the Judge who judges justly.
- In fact, this turns our natural response into something completely different. When we know the consequences of sin, we will have a concern for the souls of those who abuse us, and pray for them, knowing that, without Christ, they are facing a terrible eternity.

5. What qualities are Christian masters called to bring to their management of workers? Why?

- *They must treat them justly:* dealing with them in a way that is right, and corresponds to God's justice, not the world's justice.
- *They must treat them fairly.* This will include a fair reward for their labors and efforts, and also, presumably, fairness in what is expected of them.
- They must do this because they have a "Master in heaven" (4 v 1).

Additional question: Is there any difference between the motivations of masters and servants?

They are exactly the same: the lordship of Christ, our status in him, and the realities of the world to come—judgment or reward.

6. Most of us are a long way from the world of bondservants, slaves and masters. How might there be different aspects to our obedience to these commands today?

- We are rarely indentured to a single employer; although there are some situations which have greater similarities: when you are in the armed services, or have committed to a fixed-term contract as an apprentice perhaps.

- But in the normal course of regular work, we have far more freedom to push back and question our managers, and of course, the right to withdraw our labor, complain to higher management, take legal action or resign if we feel we are being abused or misused in some way.
- But the motivation for the way we conduct ourselves at work has not changed, nor has the godliness with which we are called to conduct ourselves changed. So even if we are put in the position where we must make some kind of protest, we must do it in a godly and respectful way.

7. How might 4:5-6 help us in the way we relate to non-Christian colleagues and managers?

- God's judgment is coming: "making the best use of the time" is not about being efficient and punctual, but about realizing that the time we are in is the era of the gospel, between Jesus' resurrection and his return, when salvation is on offer.
- So witness at work is vitally important. We should work at speaking graciously, acting wisely and speaking winsomely so that we are able to create opportunities for sharing the gospel (see the devotionalson this passage for Session 4, on page 81 of the Handbook).

Apply

FOR YOURSELF: Make a list of what your real motivations are for work. Try to be brutally honest about all the things that motivate you. If you are able to rank them, all the better.

FOR YOUR CHURCH: Where do the motivations we have discovered in today's Bible study fit in? In what practical ways can we encourage ourselves and each other to bring them higher up the list?

- Note that there are lots of other great Christian motivations for work: to provide for your family; to fulfill the creation commands of God; to use the gifts that God has given you for the flourishing of society; for the mutual support and encouragement of others; for the opportunity to evangelize.
- There are some more "neutral" motivations for work; the fun of working with others; an escape from boredom and inactivity; for the sheer love of the job itself. None of these are wrong to enjoy, but they might not add up to a valid reason for giving yourself to a particular job.
- But there are also lots of other less great motivations for our work: for self-promotion, or for seeking our own glory, or to have others affirm us, or for the chance to throw our weight around.
- We encourage ourselves by allowing the word of Christ to dwell in us richly; by reflecting on and being reminded that we are new people in Christ.
- We encourage each other when we remind each other of those truths, and when we rebuke and admonish one another when we find ourselves slipping back into "old life" ways of thinking.

Pray

FOR YOURSELF: Pray that God would give you the right attitude as a worker or as a manager. Ask the Lord to help you be respectful, hard-working and focused on serving him in your daily occupation. Ask for opportunities to share the gospel at work.

FOR YOUR CHURCH: Pray that you would encourage one another to live the new life that the gospel brings—especially in your attitudes toward work. Pray that there would be a loving spirit of mutual encouragement.

FURTHER READING

Most people seek God in mystical experiences, spectacular miracles, and extraordinary acts they have to do. To find him in vocation brings him, literally, down to earth, makes us see how close he really is to us, and transfigures everyday life.
Gene Veith

I long to accomplish a great and and noble task, but it is my chief duty to accomplish humble tasks as though they were great and noble.
Helen Keller

You work for Jesus. That fact is the most important thing you can know and remember about your work.
Sebastian Traeger & Greg Gilbert

Books

- *The Bible Speaks Today Commentary: Colossians & Philemon (Dick Lucas)*
- *Every Good Endeavor, part three (Timothy Keller with Katherine Leary Alsdorf)*
- *Time for Every Thing? (Matt Fuller)*
- *1 Peter For You, chapters seven and eight (Juan Sanchez)*
- *The Stories We Tell (Mike Cosper)*

Online

- *How to Witness at Work: gospelshapedchurch.org/resources451*
- *How the Gospel Prepares your Heart for Work (video): gospelshapedchurch.org/resources452*
- *Applying Scripture to your Work (video): gospelshapedchurch.org/resources453*
- *What Makes Work "Christian"? gospelshapedchurch.org/resources454*
- *How to Build a Faithful Witness in your Workplace: gospelshapedchurch.org/resources455*

LEADER'S REFLECTIONS

SESSION 6:

WORK AND POWER

ALL OF US HAVE SOME POWER AS WE DO OUR WORK.
WE ALL SHAPE OTHERS, AND OUR SURROUNDINGS,
FOR BETTER AND FOR WORSE. IN THIS SESSION,
YOU'LL BE INSPIRED AND CHALLENGED TO BRING
CHRISTIAN JOY AND HOPE TO THE PLACES WHERE
YOU GO AND THE WAYS IN WHICH YOU WORK.

TALK OUTLINE

6.1 • Describe the TV show *"Undercover Boss."* It shines a light on the dignity of *all* work, whether you're a CEO or cleaning windows. The Bible says the same thing.
- Israel was supposed to be a place of peace, plenty, righteousness, security and rest, with God at its center—but the people turned their backs on him.
- As punishment, God caused the Babylonians to defeat and capture the Israelites.
- Jeremiah 29 is God's letter to the exiles. What he says is unexpected…

6.2 • **SEEK THE WELFARE OF THE CITY** *Jeremiah 29:4-14*
"Welfare" = **shalom** (v 7): a life of rich abundant blessings under the loving rule of God. God tells his people to work for the common good of Babylon. So we should:

(1) Seek the common good. In Genesis 1, the garden was a place of flourishing. Christians should seek the good of others (1 Thessalonians 5:15). It is an expression of our peace in Christ. It is how we love our neighbor.

(2) Steward your power. Jeremiah 29 is addressed to conquered people—yet there is an expectation that they will bless the community. Every person has some level of influence over others—an ability to make others' lives better. How can you bring the love, joy and *shalom* of Jesus into your workplace? How can you shine the light of the gospel with your actions and words (Matthew 5:16)?

6.3 • **FOUR WAYS TO USE OUR INFLUENCE**
- **Bloom where you are planted:** Think about how your work can glorify God. Strive to consciously rely on God in your daily work; seek his help in prayer.
- **Donate your skills:** Maybe at church, or in the wider community.
- **Invent:** What are the needs in your community? Invent a way to meet them.
- **Invest:** Invest as a church in tackling a specific issue in your community. As a church and as individuals, we can invest in job-creating businesses and products.
Does all this sound nice but unrealistic? Jeremiah 29:11-12 is a powerful encouragement. God desires *shalom* and has good plans for his creation.

• **CONCLUSION:** All of us have influence and power through our work to serve the common good.

You can download a full transcript of these talks at
WWW.GOSPELSHAPEDCHURCH.ORG/WORK/TALKS

WORK AND POWER

 **WATCH DVD 6.1** (4 min 59 sec) **OR DELIVER TALK 6.1** (see page 126)

* Encourage the group to make notes as they watch the DVD or listen to the talk. There is space for notes on page 113 of the Handbook.

Discuss

READ JEREMIAH 29:4-14

> [4] Thus says the Lord of hosts, the God of Israel, to all the exiles whom I have sent into exile from Jerusalem to Babylon: [5] Build houses and live in them; plant gardens and eat their produce. [6] Take wives and have sons and daughters; take wives for your sons, and give your daughters in marriage, that they may bear sons and daughters; multiply there, and do not decrease. [7] But seek the welfare of the city where I have sent you into exile, and pray to the Lord on its behalf, for in its welfare you will find your welfare. [8] For thus says the Lord of hosts, the God of Israel: Do not let your prophets and your diviners who are among you deceive you, and do not listen to the dreams that they dream, [9] for it is a lie that they are prophesying to you in my name; I did not send them, declares the Lord.
>
> [10] For thus says the Lord: When seventy years are completed for Babylon, I will visit you, and I will fulfill to you my promise and bring you back to this place. [11] For I know the plans I have for you, declares the Lord, plans for welfare and not for evil, to give you a future and a hope. [12] Then you will call upon me and come and pray to me, and I will hear you. [13] You will seek me and find me, when you seek me with all your heart. [14] I will be found by you, declares the Lord, and I will restore your fortunes and gather you from all the nations and all the places where I have driven you, declares the Lord, and I will bring you back to the place from which I sent you into exile.

What surprises you about what God says to these exiles? What might you have expected him to say?

God tells his people to settle in Babylon and make it their home. They are to:
- build houses and plant gardens (v 5).
- make sure their families continue to grow by marrying and having children, who are to grow up and do the same (v 6). *
- "seek the welfare of the city" by how they live and what they pray (v 7).
- do this for seventy years, after which God will bring them out of Babylon and back to the land of Israel (v 10).

King Nebuchadnezzar had captured the Israelites and taken them into exile in Babylon (Jeremiah 29:1; Daniel 1:1-2). The Babylonians were the enemies of the Israelites, so we might have expected God to tell his people to have nothing to do with them, and even to undermine them when possible. But God tells them the opposite instead.

*NOTE: The command in verse 6 to take wives will have meant wives from within the Israelite community. God had made it very clear elsewhere that his people are not to marry those of other faiths (eg: Exodus 34:16; 1 Kings 11:1-4; Nehemiah 13:23-27).

What do you think it means to "seek the welfare" of a city (v 7)?

You may want to explain to the group that the word translated as "welfare" in this passage is the Hebrew word *shalom*. This word is often translated as "peace," but it means more than that. As we have seen in previous sessions, *shalom* means wholeness, peace and flourishing. It means a return to the goodness found in the Garden of Eden. So, to "seek the welfare" of a city means to work toward wholeness and goodness for everyone in that city. It means seeking peace and flourishing for the Babylonians who live there as well as for the Israelite exiles.

Why do you think God wants Israel to seek the welfare of Babylon?

You may want to point the group to the end of verse 7: "for in its welfare you will find your welfare." The Israelites are going to spend seventy years living in Babylon, so the welfare of the city will directly affect their own welfare.

But seeking the welfare of Babylon is about more than just ensuring the welfare of the Israelites who are living there. The way God's people live should point to the truth about God himself, as they live as "images" of him (Genesis

1:26-27). As these exiles live out what it means to be God's people, they will be reflecting God's character and love to those around them. This, too, will contribute to the welfare, wholeness and flourishing of Babylon.

▶ **WATCH DVD 6.2** (5 min 53 sec) **OR DELIVER TALK 6.2** (see page 126)

* *Encourage the group to make notes as they watch the DVD or listen to the talk. There is space for notes on page 115 of the Handbook.*

Discuss

In what ways do you think you might have influence in your workplace? How might you use that influence to seek the common good with your work, and in your workplace?

Everyone has the potential to influence their workplace, even if they do not have any kind of leadership role. If people struggle to see how they can have influence, try asking the question in a different way: "How can you make someone else's life better?" Answers could include the way we make someone a coffee, not grumbling when something goes wrong, how we greet people in the morning, looking out for ways to help others, remembering birthdays and anniversaries, etc. There are also "bigger picture" answers to this question. We can encourage our companies to be more ethical in their business behavior, more energy efficient, and more connected with the local community.

👉 **READ 1 THESSALONIANS 5:15**

See that no one repays anyone evil for evil, but always seek to do good to one another and to everyone.

What do you think *"seeking the common good"* should look like in your local community?

Try to keep this discussion specific to your local neighborhood. What needs do people have? How could you begin to meet some of those needs?

What is your workplace currently doing that contributes to the common good? What else could your workplace be doing?

The answers to this question will vary greatly according to what each person's current occupation is. Those who work alone, or who are stay-at-home parents, or retired or unemployed may need some prompting to think of answers. You may want to think about this beforehand so that you are ready to make suggestions for anyone who finds it hard to think of anything they currently do or could do that can contribute to the common good.

▶ **WATCH DVD 6.3** (5 min 43 sec) **OR DELIVER TALK 6.3** (see page xx)

* *Encourage the group to make notes as they watch the DVD or listen to the talk. There is space for notes on page xx of the Handbook.*

Discuss

In the last few sessions we have been thinking about ways in which we can glorify God or serve God in our work; in other words, how we can "bloom where we are planted." Have you defined what some of these ways are for you personally? How have you been reminding yourself about them as you have gone about your work in the past couple of weeks?

This is an opportunity to recap some of the discussions from previous weeks. If some of your group members have not yet put any of their ideas into action, think about how you can encourage them to do that this week. Can individuals contact each other during the week to see how they are getting on?

Three possible ways of using your influence wisely are to 1) donate your skills, 2) invent, or 3) invest. Choose one of these and think about how you might do this in your own workplace.

1) **Donate your skills:** God has gifted each one of us with a skill set and experience. How can we use these as a Christian influence for good in our workplace, or in the wider community?

2) **Invent:** Is there a need or opportunity in your community that isn't being addressed? How can we take the initiative to start something new in this area?

3) **Invest:** Do we have time, money or energy that we can invest in some way in our community? Maybe on our own, or maybe in combination with others.

Now think about how your church family can together seek the common good of your local community. Is there an issue that you could donate your combined skills to, invent a solution to between you, or invest in together? How might you start to do this?

This is an opportunity to think together about a way in which your church family can work together for the benefit of the local neighborhood. You will also want to decide how to follow through with your idea, eg: who will take responsibility for it, or for suggesting it to your church leadership?

Pray

"In the same way, let your light shine before others, so that they may see your good works and give glory to your Father who is in heaven."

Think about any non-Christians who see you in your daily workplace. Ask God to help you to live for him in such a way that "your light shines" before them, and they praise God as a result.

"For I know the plans I have for you, declares the Lord, plans for welfare and not for evil, to give you a future and a hope. Then you will call upon me and come and pray to me, and I will hear you. You will seek me and find me, when you seek me with all your heart."

Use these verses as the basis on which to pray for yourself, your workplace and your church.

DAILY BIBLE DEVOTIONALS

This week's daily Bible devotionals take us through the life in Babylonian exile of Daniel, Shadrach, Meshach and Abednego in Daniel 1 – 7, demonstrating how God's people are to live and work in a world that does not know him; and showing how our conduct at work is connected to our doctrine of God.

SERMONS

OPTION ONE: JEREMIAH 29:4-14

This passage is the one Tom focuses on in the main session, which could be expanded upon in a sermon.

OPTION TWO: MARK 10:32-45

This is the passage the Bible study is based on (see next page), which could also be expanded upon in a sermon.

OPTION THREE: PROVERBS 31

Compare the approach to work, and blessing given through their work, of:
- King Lemuel, who used his power to pursue sex and excess, rather than justice for the powerless (v 2-9),
- and the "excellent wife," who, though stewarding far less power than a king, worked hard, prudently, creatively and selflessly, and was therefore a blessing to those around her, and particularly her husband and children (v 10-31).

OPTION FOUR: GALATIANS 5:22 - FAITHFULNESS AT WORK

Church members will find a page to write notes on the sermon on page 129 of their Handbooks.

 **BIBLE STUDY**

AIM: The main session raises the idea that Christians should be working to bless the world with their work. We all have "vocational power" to influence others, to make our workplaces more positive places, to spread *shalom* in the world. In this study we will look at Jesus' teaching on how Christians are to use their power and authority.

Discuss

Have you ever met someone who is really "important"—either because of their position, or something they achieved? What did it feel like for you to meet them? How did they behave? How do you feel about them now?

Let people tell their stories about meeting "a great one." Some will have been nervous and tongue tied. Some may have stories about how the person they met was kind, humble and easy to speak to. Others may have been disappointed to meet someone who seemed dismissive or self important, or even arrogant.

 READ MARK 10:32-45

Jesus said:
44 Whoever would be great among you must be your servant, and whoever would be first among you must be slave of all. 45 For even the Son of Man came not to be served but to serve, and to give his life as a ransom for many.

An extraordinary scene unfolds—Jesus is striding along the road to Jerusalem with purpose and resolution; the disciples are following behind, some amazed, more of them terrified about what is about to happen. Then he turns to explain to them what is going on...

1. **What does Jesus tell his disciples? Why is it so amazing that Jesus tells them this at this particular moment (Hint: Think about what he is doing as he speaks, v 22)?**
   - Jesus knows that people will spit on him, laugh at him, flog him and kill him. But in the end he will rise again from the dead.

- He knows all this, and yet he walks purposefully toward Jerusalem. He says yes to the cross, because it is the only way to bring forgiveness to the world. He says yes to suffering and pain, for the glory that lies beyond.

Additional question: What is the principle of the Christian life that he implies by this statement?

Suffering before glory. The way of Christian service is one where we expect to work and suffer now, in the hope of eternal glory with Jesus.

2. **What are James and John asking for in verse 37? What do you think about the way that they make their request?**

- They want to be the top two people in Jesus' kingdom.
- They are being quite sneaky and manipulative about it. They want him to agree to their request before he knows what it is, and before the other disciples discover what is going on.

3. **What is the meaning of the questions that Jesus asks them in v 36? What does their answer to him reveal about their understanding of his mission, and the statement he made in v 33-34?**

- Jesus asks them whether they can drink the cup he drinks. This is the cup of suffering and God's wrath.
- The baptism that Jesus refers to is a picture of the suffering and death he must go through.
- James and John simply do not get it. They enthusiastically say they can do those things, but do not understand what they are asking for. At this point they do not understand what Jesus' mission is in the world, and they do not understand the true nature of Jesus' kingship and work.
- The Lord has been painfully specific in v 33-34 about what will happen to him, but somehow they still think that serving in Jesus' kingdom will be an experience of wonderful peace and the wielding of power in a righteous way.

4. **What does Jesus promise them life will be like in his service (v 39-40)? Why are we so attracted to versions of Christianity which seem to promise us comfort, ease and success?**

- He makes it clear that as his followers they will experience the same rejection, misunderstanding and persecution that he will receive in Jerusalem.
- We would love to embrace a Christian faith that means we will enjoy health, wealth and success—the popularity of preachers who promise these things is testament to the power of this (false) message.
- We are attracted to it because we naturally lean away from suffering, assuming that it is bad for us.
- But in genuine Christianity, suffering and service seem to be the means by which God achieves wonderful things in our world—the salvation Jesus won on the cross is the model for our own lives.
- Suffering is also a way that we can grow as Christians.

5. **What is the fundamental attitude toward power that Jesus wants his followers to embody? How is this different from the way power is used in the world (see verses 42-45)?**

- Greatness in the kingdom of God is achieved by serving. Notice that Jesus says a "slave of all." The kind of humble servitude he is calling us to is wide ranging and without limits.
- We must be humble and willing to use our gifts, responsibilities and power to serve others, not ourselves.
- This is completely different to how the world tends to work—where people often use their power and privilege to serve themselves, and to seek glory for themselves, rather than to wield their power for the benefit of others.

NOTE: That is not to say that the world *always* uses its power in this way. There will be some generous-hearted and humble people who are not Christian, but whose attitude in work commands loyalty and hard work because they are displaying attractive Christ-like qualities—even though they are not seeking to follow him.

- Christians show this quality in their lives because they are followers of Jesus. And verse 45 makes it clear that this is what Jesus did in coming to live and die for his people.

6. **How should this principle be worked out in church structures and relationships? How far is it legitimate to take this principle for Christian living into our daily work? Are there any limitations on how this should be applied to our work in the world?**

- In church life, we will always have a relatively "flat" structure of responsibilities and relationships. We are all one in Christ Jesus and we are called to serve each other.
- No one will consider themselves better or greater than another, because we are all at bottom sinners saved by grace.
- There is a hierarchy of respect and calling—those who teach and lead and serve as leaders (deacons and elders) are to be honored and provided for. But that does not alter our common standing and our need to be subject to one another.
- Part of this attitude will also mark how we relate at work to both Christians and "not-yet-Christians" (see *Gospel Shaped Outreach*). Now we look at no one from a human point of view. The very highest person in your organization and the very lowest person are humans made in the image of God, who are at base sinners in need of God's grace and forgiveness.
- If we are responsible for managing people, we will want to understand that relationship, at least in part, as a call to serve them, as they serve the needs of the organization.
- When we use our power in a way that is distinctive from others, we will model the love and grace of Christ, and witness to his transforming power.
- We must be careful not to allow this attitude to be misused at work, however. We still have fundamental responsibilities to fulfill at work. People must be managed, encouraged and rebuked as appropriate. It does not mean we will be a doormat, or easily manipulated.

Additional question: How ambitious should Christians be to be promoted in their work and to seek greater power within an organization, do you think?

- Allow the group to discuss this question for which there is no right or wrong answer. But try to focus on the motivations. We can seek power to make the workplace a more healthy environment, so that people are treated better. And we can seek more power to shape the direction of the company toward something more wholesome and fulfilling of God's creation commands.

- But we should beware conflicts of interest with our other responsibilities at home, church and in the community.

Apply

FOR YOURSELF: What power do you have—at home, in church and at work? How do you wield it—as a Christ-like servant, or as a self-centered leader? Can you think of one thing you can do that will help you serve in a more Christ-like way this week?

FOR YOUR CHURCH: Does your church have a culture of honesty, where people can share how they are struggling—or is there a general feeling that everyone is coping and doing well? How might you be part of the way in which your church becomes a more nurturing place for people who may be suffering in silence at the moment?

Pray

FOR YOU AND YOUR GROUP: Spend some time praising your Savior for his perseverance in the face of ultimate suffering. Thank the Lord that he became a servant so that we could be ransomed from slavery to sin and death. Pray that you would increasingly grow like him in humble service of one another.

FOR YOUR WORK: Pray for your individual working situations, and for the power that you have over others. Ask God for wisdom in how you express and use your power with others.

FOR THE CHURCH THROUGHOUT THE WORLD: Pray for your brothers and sisters worldwide who are facing hostile opposition every day—experiencing the "cup" and "baptism" of the Lord Jesus. Pray that those who are persecuted would continue to trust Jesus; that they would look to him, and persevere to his praise and glory. And pray that your own church, and particularly your leadership, would be models of humble service.

FURTHER READING

We are not to choose jobs and conduct our work to fulfill ourselves and accrue power ... we are to see work as a way of service to God and our neighbor.
Timothy Keller

When God grants us power—and he does in many ways—his aim is that he will be glorified by the way that power is used.
John Piper

Books

- *Living in the Light: Money, Sex & Power (John Piper)*
- *Rescuing Ambition (Dave Harvey)*
- *Generous Justice (Timothy Keller)*

Online

- *5 Ways to Help the "Least of These" in the Church: gospelshapedchurch.org/resources461*
- *Is Your Gospel Too Small? gospelshapedchurch.org/resources462*
- *The One Who Showed Mercy: gospelshapedchurch.org/resources463*
- *To Quit or Not to Quit: gospelshapedchurch.org/resources464*
- *Humanizing Work Through Leadership (video): gospelshapedchurch.org/resources365*

LEADER'S REFLECTIONS

SESSION 7:

WORK AND THE COMMON GOOD

THIS SESSION IS ABOUT ECONOMICS – BUT NOT ONLY
NATIONAL-LEVEL QUESTIONS OF TAXATION AND
SPENDING, BUT ALSO DAY-TO-DAY, INDIVIDUAL DECISIONS
ABOUT HOW WE USE WHAT WE HAVE BEEN GIVEN.
YOU'LL LEARN TO THINK DIFFERENTLY ABOUT THE
CHOICES YOU MAKE EVERY DAY, AND HOW THEY CAN
BE SHAPED BY THE GOSPEL FOR THE GOOD OF THOSE
AROUND YOU.

TALK OUTLINE

7.1 • What do you think when you hear the word "economics"? It's important to understand economics in light of the Bible's story.

- ## WHAT DO WE MEAN BY ECONOMICS?
  Economics is: *how we choose to use scarce resources that have alternative uses.* We all make choices every day about how we use our money, time, homes, relationships, etc. We should make the best use of these resources (Ephesians 5:16).
  - **All of life is stewardship** (Psalm 24:1-2): Your job, money, time, relationships and giftedness are given to you by God. So ask: *How does he want me to use them?*
  - **We will give an account** for our stewardship (Matthew 25:14-30). Jesus is looking for fruitful followers. So ask: *Have I used the things God has given me for his glory?*

7.2 • **GOSPEL-SHAPED ECONOMICS**
The Bible shows that our economic choices should promote the common good.
- **The common good and creation.** The pattern of work for Adam and Eve involved collaboration—working together to enhance the community and expand *shalom*.
- **The common good in the Old Testament.** God's word values private property, but protects the poor (Exodus 20, Ruth); tells us to work hard and diligently (Proverbs 12:11); and tells us to seek honesty and fair exchange (Amos 8:5-6).
- **The common good and Jesus** (Luke 10:25-29). We are to love our neighbor— whoever they are. This involves Christ-like compassion and economic capacity.

7.3 • **HOW CAN OUR ECONOMICS ENCOURAGE THE COMMON GOOD?**
The Bible has significant economic implications:
- **The value of private property** (Deuteronomy 19:14), but we are simply stewards.
- **Safety from abuse of power** (16:19).
- **Dependable currency** (Amos 8), to enable secure exchange and co-operation.
- **Profit and incentive**—a system where hard work is rewarded, and so promoted.
- **Value added**—Christians are to add value to our communities, not extract it.
- **Healthy families**—our economics must support family life.
- **Care for the poor**—both on an individual level and a global scale.
My economic choices display whether I live to please myself or love my neighbor.

You can download a full transcript of these talks at
WWW.GOSPELSHAPEDCHURCH.ORG/LIVING/TALKS

WORK AND THE COMMON GOOD

NOTE: This session is a basic introduction to economic activity and decision-making, mainly regarding our personal decisions but also touching on a community and country level. Since it is introductory and just a single session, it seeks to avoid over-qualification and nuance for the sake of simplicity and application. If your group contains people who work in high-level governmental, academic or charity roles who have a grasp of large-scale economics, do remind them that this is *introductory*, and not comprehensive. Make sure the discussion does not get overly academic or complex in a way that will leave some group members behind.

▶ **WATCH DVD 7.1** (5 min 58 sec) **OR DELIVER TALK 7.1** (see page 144)

* *Encourage the group to make notes as they watch the DVD or listen to the talk. There is space for notes on page 133 of the Handbook.*

Discuss

👉 **READ MATTHEW 25:14-30**

> [16] *For [the kingdom of heaven] will be like a man going on a journey, who called his servants and entrusted to them his property ...*
>
> [19] *After a long time the master of those servants came and settled accounts with them.* [20] *And he who had received the five talents came forwards, bringing five talents more, saying, 'Master, you delivered to me five talents; here I have made five talents more.'* [21] *His master said to him, 'Well done, good and faithful servant. You have been faithful over a little; I will set you over much. Enter into the joy of your master.'*

The man going on a journey is a picture of the Lord Jesus, who left this world when he ascended to heaven, and will one day return to it in power and glory.

What should we be doing in the meantime, and how do the master's words in verses 21 and 23 motivate us to do this?

We are to use all that we have—our abilities, our time, our relationships, our opportunities and so on—in the service of the one who gave them to us, that is, Jesus. (A "talent" was a monetary unit worth around 20 years of a laborer's wages— a great deal of money!) This will take intentionality, discipline and hard work. But as we do this, we can be motivated by:

- looking forward to hearing the Lord say to us of our hard work for him: "Well done, good and faithful servant" (v 21, 23). Encourage your group to imagine how amazing it will be to hear the Lord of creation say this to us!
- looking forward to being rewarded in the kingdom of heaven with work for, and alongside, the Lord (v 21, 23), which is still greater than the privilege it is to do his work now, while he is "away."
- looking forward to knowing our Master's joy (v 21, 23). All that belongs to Jesus, he will share with us—we will experience the joy of being perfect, of living with our Father, of seeing him face to face, and so on.
- understanding that we are called to do what we can with what we have, and that Jesus says "well done" to us whether we have been given great amounts of "talents" (like the first servant, v 21) or a lesser amount (v 23). Jesus does not compare us with those to whom he has given more, or less, as we so often do; he simply asks us to do what we can with what we have been given.

How does the third servant's description of the master's character in verses 24-25 show that he misunderstood what his master was like? Was he really a servant at all?

Make sure your group are comparing this servant's attitude with the master's generosity in v 14-15, and his praise and welcome in verses 21 and 23. The master had given each servant all that they had, and the third had been given two decades' worth of salary—yet he thinks of his master as "a hard man" (v 24). The investment money belonged to the master, not the servant—yet the servant viewed the master as reaping where he had not sown, as though the talent really belonged to the servant. And the servant was afraid of the master (v 25), whereas the master was wanting to greet him as a "good" servant and share all his joy with him (v 21, 23).

The point is that this servant *does not actually know his master*. He thinks he is serving a harsh, selfish man—but the master is nothing like this! And in v 26-27, the master suggests that the third servant is a liar—in fact, he likely did not think the master would return and so lived for himself, not his master.

So in this sense, he is not really a servant of the master. He lives for himself, he does not know his master and his character and he has no relationship with him. So it is not that Jesus is warning true Christians that they must fear that, if they are not fruitful, they will be shut out of his kingdom (v 30). Rather, he is warning that those who treat God as though he will not return or is not gracious will not share Christ's joy in his kingdom. Nevertheless, the implication is that those who know Christ will return and know his grace (ie: true Christians) will be fruitful, and will view all they have as a gift from God, to be used for his glory and not for themselves.

You are in charge of an economy that has been entrusted to you by Christ— your own! What is exciting about this idea?

It is likely that, even for those who pay attention to (or work with) economics on a macro (large-scale) level, this idea of personal economics, to be directed by the gospel, is a new idea. It elevates the choices we make about how to use/ invest our God-given resources from the mundane to the eternally significant. Every personal economic choice can lead us into (or away from) greater godliness, and greater use to the gospel. So allow your group to think about and discuss what they find striking about this, and encourage them (if they need it) to connect the gospel to these areas of their everyday lives.

▶ **WATCH DVD 7.2** (4 min 42 sec) **OR DELIVER TALK 7.2** (see page 144)

* *Encourage the group to make notes as they watch the DVD or listen to the talk. There is space for notes on page 135 of the Handbook.*

Discuss

How can we, like the lawyer Jesus met, seek to limit the range of those whom we have to love? Why is this tempting?

We limit the range of who qualifies as "neighbor" whenever we believe that a particular "type" of person is less deserving of our time, attention, care or love than another. Those limits may have to do with economic status (eg: those who are unemployed), legal status (eg: illegal immigrants or felons), geographical status (those who do not live near us), religion (eg: Muslims or humanists), and so on. Our hearts find it very easy to limit the range of who we have to love because we would like to make it easier for ourselves to keep Jesus' command to "Love your neighbor" (Mark 12:31). In particular we prefer to "love" those who are like us, whom we are naturally drawn to, or who may repay us in some way—which is, of course, actually self-loving, not neighbor-loving.

What will go wrong with our day-to-day choices and bigger life choices when we forget to consider either:
• **how to live with Christ-like compassion, or**
• **that we need to live within our economic capacity.**

A lack of Christ-like compassion will see us act selfishly, or for the good only of our own family. Since we have scarce resources, time, and so on, we will use them to further our own ends and meet our own goals (whether they be comfort, promotion, wealth, relationship, etc). The parable of the Good Samaritan (Luke 10:29-37) is a lesson in how to live in the way the greatest "Good Samaritan"—the Lord Jesus—did.

A lack of understanding that we must live within our economic capacity means we will burn out or drop out. God has given each of us a certain amount of time and energy, and a particular set of circumstances. Just as Jesus slept, took time to pray, etc. (Mark 1:35; 4:38), so we need to remember that wisdom is called for—we cannot do everything. We are to be sacrificial, but to be so sustainably, so that we might continue to live with compassion tomorrow too. Wise compassion is the way in which we are to live.

▶ **WATCH DVD 7.3** (5 min 3 sec) **OR DELIVER TALK 7.3** (see page 144)

* *Encourage the group to make notes as they watch the DVD or listen to the talk. There is space for notes on page 136 of the Handbook.*

Discuss

Which of the seven biblical economic principles that Tom listed did you find most surprising? interesting? challenging?

1. **The value of private property**
2. **Safety from abuse of power**
3. **Dependable currency**
4. **Profit and incentive**
5. **Value added**
6. **Healthy families**
7. **Care for the poor**

Obviously, different members of your group will have been struck by different principles, but guide the discussion toward thinking through the aspects of each principle that you do understand, and that might change or influence your outlook, actions and prayers. Don't let this become a long discussion either about what someone doesn't understand (or disagrees strongly with), or about what you are all doing really well already!

If there is no single, one-size-fits-all biblical economics, how should that affect the way we view politics, and the way we treat those with whom we disagree on economic or political issues?

Again, don't let the discussion get drawn into a political debate. The important thing is to realize that when a Christian disagrees with us on an area of economics (eg: how involved the state should be in caring for the poor; whether the tax system should be progressive; whether a government should protect jobs by imposing import duties), they are most likely not being ungodly. We should hold our own position humbly, and treat others respectfully, rather than demonizing them; and we should remember that it is our wise application of Christ-like compassion that matters most.

Care needs to be taken in leading this discussion as the group may easily get confused about which parts of the Bible Christians should aim to apply to the state, and which apply primarily to the church. Worshiping idols, for example, is roundly condemned as a sin throughout Scripture. This sin should be preached against in church and church members pastored and disciplined when they fall into idolatry of various kinds. But this does not mean that believers should be campaigning for idolatry to be made illegal in our pluralistic society.

As thoughtful students of the Bible we see that economics is first and foremost about creating blessing from the created order. Tom summarized economics as being *"how we choose to use scarce resources that have alternative uses."* What economic decisions will you face this week? How has this session empowered and challenged you about those economic choices?

The purpose of this question is to finish by applying what you have heard and discussed to your individual lives in a positive way. Encourage your group to be specific and practical, and (if this is the first time they have thought about these issues in this way) to keep considering how they can glorify God in the way they use the resources he has given them.

Pray

"Well done, good and faithful servant. You have been faithful over a little; I will set you over much. Enter into the joy of your master."

Thank the Lord for the joy that lies before his people. Thank him for the prospect of hearing these words said in welcome to each of you.

Thank him for the particular time, energy, abilities and circumstances he has given you, and pray for yourself and the others in your group for the compassion and wisdom to know how best to serve him in how you use those gifts.

Thank God for those in your church who exemplify God-directed, God-glorifying daily choices with their "talents."

DAILY BIBLE DEVOTIONALS

These six devotionals look at how the gospel transforms our view on and use of money, by studying how meeting Jesus changed Zacchaeus, and then looking at Paul's cautions and exhortations about wealth in 1 Timothy 6:6-19.

SERMONS

OPTION ONE: MATTHEW 25:14-30

This passage is one that Tom looks at in the main session, but which could very helpfully be further expounded upon in a sermon.

OPTION TWO: JAMES 4:13 – 5:6

This is the passage the Bible study is based on (see next page), which could also be expanded upon in a sermon.

OPTION THREE: 2 CORINTHIANS 8 – 9

- Gospel-motivated giving is sacrificial, voluntary and joyful (8:1-5)
- Our decisions about our money are to be made based on an understanding and love of the grace of God in Christ (8:9), a reliance on the ongoing provision of God (9:8-11), and a desire for God to be glorified (9:12-14).

OPTION FOUR: GALATIANS 5:23 – GENTLENESS AT WORK

Church members will find a page to write notes on the sermon on page 149 of their Handbooks.

BIBLE STUDY

AIM: The main session focused on exploring ideas about economics in the world: both our own personal choices, and larger ones that affect our local communities, and national and international perspectives. There is a place for thinking about how the gospel interacts with "big picture" economics—but this study focuses on a couple of very real areas of economic choice that we all face day by day: how we choose to spend our time, and how we choose to spend our money! It may be appropriate to remind your group members of the definition of economics that Tom gave on the DVD: *"how we choose to use scarce resources that have alternative uses."*

Discuss

If someone looked at your daily or weekly calendar, or the things you thought important to list in your diary, what might they conclude about what is really important to you?

You might ask people to bring in their calendars; read out a selection of these to see if people can guess whose calendar it is. The general discussion might touch on how we tend to diarize important meetings, but not diarize prayer, or church or Bible reading. It may show how we do not set relational priorities— ie: diarizing time to spend with our spouse/children/friends.

READ JAMES 4:13 – 5:6

¹⁷ *Whoever knows the right thing to do and fails to do it, for him it is sin.*

James is writing a book of "gospel-shaped wisdom" for Christians living in the real world. In this passage he focuses our attention on the choices we make in using two scarce resources: time and money!

1. **Who is James speaking to in these verses (4:13)? What does their priority appear to be?**

In the most specific sense, James is speaking to people who make plans regarding travel and business. In James' day, merchants would have spent time in a new place establishing contacts and trading before moving on somewhere else. But really, verse 13 is simply talking to people who make plans more generally—the details may differ, but plans like this are part and parcel of most of our lives. We all make plans and think a year or so ahead—so he is speaking to us! The priority of James' readers is to "carry on business and make money." Profit is the motive for the planning. Again, this is not very different from the priorities of many of us today.

2. **What perspectives does James say gospel-shaped people should have, which will drive them to make different choices (v 14, 15)?**

- *The future:* We "do not even know what will happen tomorrow" (v 14a). None of us know what the immediate future holds. We are not in control of it, however much planning we do. We may put arrangements into the schedule as if they are a given (business trip, family holiday, seeing friends, starting a project), but James reminds us that we cannot simply assume that once we've planned something, it will happen. We don't know the future.
- *Our lives:* We are just "a mist that appears for a little while and then vanishes." Although we are made in the image of God, "a little lower than angels", and are deeply loved by God, our lives are fragile and vulnerable! James is reminding us that actually, in the grand scheme of things, we are not the center of the universe, and we should not imagine ourselves to be so.
- *God is sovereign:* "If it is the Lord's will, we will live and do this or that." James is telling these people (and us) that there is nothing wrong with planning; but we shouldn't plan in a way that forgets that God sovereignly overrules our lives. James is not telling us to add a mindless platitude to everything ("If it's God's will…") but to plan in a way that recognizes and remembers that we are not in ultimate control, and that all our plans are subject to the will of God; and that we are not the center of the universe or the most important person: God is.
- It means having a mindset which is ruled not by our personal ambition and greed, but by a knowledge of and submission to God's will for our lives. Note that God's will for our lives as revealed in Scripture is for us to grow more like Christ.

3. **How does verse 15 help us to see why the attitude of verse 13 is, as James puts it, "arrogant", "boasting" and "evil" (v 16)?**

- It is an arrogant view because it sees the future as under control, and the self as at the center.
- It is "boasting" because it makes them more important than they really are…
- and so it is "evil" because it forgets who God is. What seemed innocuous, sensible planning in verse 13 actually betrays an attitude that is vain, even "evil". This is very challenging to realize because often our planning is exactly like that of verse 13.

4. **Why is it good news that God is in charge of the future? How should these verses affect both how we plan, and what we plan?**

- It is great news that there is someone in control, and that we know him to be both all-knowing and completely loving. And it is even greater news when we consider that God's purpose is to use our circumstances to make us more like Christ (1:3-5; Romans 8:28), and that he will definitely bring us through everything that lies in our future to bring us home to him (1:12; see Philippians 1:6). The purpose of this question is to help your group realize that God's control of our future is not oppressive, but liberating and encouraging.
- **How we plan:** We will plan prayerfully and humbly, bearing in mind that God may direct our life differently, and asking him to help us to plan in a way that makes the wisest use of the time and opportunities he's given us.
- **What we plan:** In the example of planning that James gives in verse 13, the planner's main aim is making money. Profit is the priority that drives the planning. It is not that making money is bad. It is what merchants do, after all. We would expect nothing different. But this is the point; if our planning is no different from that of the world around us, what does that say about our faith in Christ? It is not wrong for making some money to be a goal in life—we are to support ourselves and help others. But it is wrong for it to be our main goal in life. Our plans need to reflect not only the existence of God's will, but its content too. We need to make plans that enable us to do the "good" we're called to do (v 17). So if our plans mean that we are irregular in church attendance, or have no time to care for the vulnerable, or rarely listen to God in his word, then there must be some sin in our planning.

Additional question: How legitimate is it for us to apply this principle to our working lives if we work for a larger company, and do not have the power to change the goals of our organization?

Most of us will work at jobs in organizations that require us to be part of something that is worldly and far from ideal. Most companies are focused on making profit for the owners. We are not accountable for the motivation of those who run the organization—but we can focus on any greater goal our organization is striving to achieve which can be part of God's good purposes for work in the world. For instance, you may have to plan a sales trip for which the company goal is to sell products and make money; as a Christian, you can focus on what will come out of the use of these products as the primary aim, eg: healthier working environment, more efficient work, more eco-friendly energy use, etc. Even though a company's motivation may be sinful, God is still working in and through the organization to do his work in the world.

5. Who is James speaking to in 5:1-6? And what does he warn them about?

"You rich people" (v 1). There is good reason for thinking James is addressing non-Christian rich people. Notice that he does not address those he's speaking to as "brothers and sisters" or "fellow believers," which he does liberally through the rest of the letter. And there is no call to repent and return to the Lord, but only a promise of judgment.

NOTE: Why would James address the unbelieving rich, since they won't be in a church to hear his words?! Because (as the prophets often did) James is not wanting to teach those he is addressing, but to show his Christian hearers what God thinks of those he is addressing. In other words, James wants Christians to know how to think of the rich people around them in a godly way, while at the same time warning them of the thinking that belongs to the world, and which Christians are always in danger of slipping back into.

- **v 2-3:** They have amassed and hoarded wealth for its own sake, rather than using their wealth for good. But it has not done them any good, and it "testifies against" them—it exposes the sinfulness of hearts that aimed simply to *have* wealth, rather than to *use* wealth. Remind the group of the parable of the talents, which we thought about in the main session.
- **v 4:** They have used their wealth to take advantage of and exploit others, and God sees and cares about that (see also v 6).

- **v 3b, 5:** They have done all this "in the last days." In other words, the day of God's judgment is coming and is not far off, and yet they have lived for possessions in the here and now. Like turkeys eating well in October, but heading all the while for Christmas, so living for wealth now and treading on others to get more of it simply means people have "fattened [themselves] in the day of slaughter" (v 5).

6. How might we end up living like the people James takes aim at here?

- As we've seen, James is speaking principally to non-Christian wealthy people—but it is very easy for us to treat wealth in a non-Christian way, rather than ensuring that our faith impacts our deeds in this area.
- *Hoarding:* In the West, we live in a society where accumulation is seen as good in its own right. Amassing money and possessions is commended. It is one of the ways that we as a culture measure someone's success in life. The more you have, the better you've done. The things we have are a matter of pride to many of us, rather than seen as something that we are to use to bless others.
- *Injustice:* We may not be negligent landowners, as these people evidently were, but this still hits home. It is all too easy for the wealthy to overlook the needs of others and their responsibility to them. Affluence can lead to carelessness and insensitivity. Moreover, those of us in the comparative wealth of the West need to reflect on our responsibility as consumers—to think about the kinds of companies we're supporting and how they treat their workers in far-flung and impoverished places. Willful ignorance really is no defence. Our purchasing habits might well be furthering forms of injustice, and we have an opportunity to make a difference through the choices that we make. It is incumbent on us to care about such things and to do all we can to support upright companies and avoid those that deliberately hurt and exploit the economically vulnerable.
- *Extravagance:* The Bible does not say we cannot enjoy good things (see 1 Timothy 4 v 1-5). But we are not to aim for the most comfortable, pampered life possible; nor should we live envying the rich for their extravagance.

7. **What has James taught us about what "godly" economics is? What aspect did you find most challenging or thought-provoking?**

- Some will focus on more individual things, whereas others may choose to talk about how these individual principles might translate into larger themes for community, corporate, national or international economic choices.
- Don't allow the conversation to become a platform for any group member to ride an economic "hobby horse."

Apply

FOR YOURSELF: It is very easy for us to make plans or use our money without reference to God's priorities for life and his loving control over all things. How can you be more prayerful and godly in your planning and spending? When do you most need to remember consciously to bring these perspectives to mind?

FOR YOUR CHURCH: How can you cultivate conversations about these subjects that will encourage others to be godly in their decision-making? We are often very private about our spending choices, but also fearful that others will judge us for extravagance. How easy would you find it to rebuke or admonish a brother or sister for something they chose to spend their time and money on that might be unwise or unhelpful?

Pray

FOR YOUR GROUP: Ask the Lord to help you be honest about your own weaknesses and failures with each other, and that you would deal with each other gently and lovingly. Pray that you would be able to encourage each other to make good choices in the use of your time and money.

FOR YOUR CHURCH: Pray that your leaders would help church members grow in godliness and in the way you use yours time and money. Pray for a growing sense that our loving Lord is sovereign over all things.

 FURTHER READING

*We have always known that heedless self-interest was bad morals;
we now know that it is bad economics.*
Franklin D. Roosevelt

*There simply isn't time to do everything that we desire. There really isn't time to
do every thing. But there is time for everything God wants us to do. His to-do list
does get done. Can you see what an exhilarating and liberating truth this is?*
Matt Fuller

Books

- *Economic Shalom (John Bolt)*
- *The Poverty of Nations (Wayne Grudem & Barry Asmus)*
- *What's Best Next (Matt Perman)*
- *Living in the Light: Money, Sex & Power (John Piper)*
- *Money Counts (Graham Beynon)*

Online

- Cultivating Gospel Readiness at Work: gospelshapedchurch.org/resources471
- Amazon: Easy to Critique, Easier to One-Click:
  gospelshapedchurch.org/resources472
- Why All Christians Must Seek Public Justice:
  gospelshapedchurch.org/resources473
- Why Business Matters to God (video):
  gospelshapedchurch.org/resources474

LEADER'S REFLECTIONS

SESSION 8:

WHAT WE ARE WORKING TOWARD

IN OUR FIRST SESSION WE LOOKED BACK AT THE CREATION OF THE WORLD. IN THIS LAST SESSION, WE LOOK FORWARD TO THE RE-CREATION OF THE WORLD — AND AS WE DO SO, WE'LL FIND MUCH MOTIVATION TO WORK HARD, WELL AND JOYFULLY IN OUR PRESENT.

TALK OUTLINE

8.1 ● What will eternity be like? Perhaps surprisingly, in the new creation **we will work!**

8.2 ● **AN "EARTHLY" HEAVEN** *Revelation 21:1-5; 22:1-5*
The Bible speaks of a **physical place** for humans to live in resurrection bodies:
- 21:2 depicts heaven coming down to earth—not us going "up" to heaven.
- 21:5 says that God is making "all things new," not making all new things.
- There will be a "holy city" where God dwells with his people and where they will live in peace and community. Cities are part of the expansion and flourishing of humankind (mandated in Genesis 1).

This new creation has **implications for our work** (Isaiah 65:21-25):
- Good work in this world—for peace, healing, justice, etc.—will last into eternity.
- Those who feel stuck in a dreary and meaningless job here and now will one day finally taste the full fruit of their God-given talents and capacities (v 21-22).

8.3 ● **REIGNING WITH CHRIST** *Revelation 22:3-5*
- **Our work in the new creation:** Work is intrinsic to the human design (Genesis 1). In the new creation we will work for the extension of Christ's perfect kingdom into the whole universe.
- **Our work will be better**—the frustrations of work in this world will be gone.

● **GOSPEL SHAPED WORK**
How does the gospel story shape our view of work? In this series we've seen:
(1) Creation. We're created to work. We're called to honor work, enjoy it, embrace it and give ourselves to it.
(2) The fall. We live under the curse of the fall—so it's not surprising when work is difficult or exhausting.
(3) Redemption. Christ is redeeming people, our world and our work—so we work with a new perspective.
(4) New creation. We will work in the new creation and reign with Christ forever.

● **CONCLUSION:** Jesus is calling you to be part of that new creation. How will that transform the way you work?

You can download a full transcript of these talks at
WWW.GOSPELSHAPEDCHURCH.ORG/WORK/TALKS

WHAT WE ARE WORKING TOWARD

Discuss

What are the primary images our culture uses to think about heaven?

When you think about eternity, what pictures come to your mind? Which do you find the most appealing or attractive?

These opening questions will lead into the first section of the DVD.

▶ **WATCH DVD 8.1** (2 min 2 sec) **OR DELIVER TALK 8.1** (see page 162)

* *Encourage the group to make notes as they watch the DVD or listen to the talk. There is space for notes on page 153 of the Handbook.*

Discuss

"In the new creation, we will work." How do you react to this statement?

Some in your group may be surprised—or disappointed—to hear that they will be working in the new creation. Others may be looking forward to it, or intrigued to find out what kind of work they may be doing. The rest of this session will unpack these ideas further.

☞ **READ REVELATION 21:1-5 AND 22:1-5**

> [1] *Then I saw a new heaven and a new earth, for the first heaven and the first earth had passed away, and the sea was no more. [2] And I saw the holy city, new Jerusalem, coming down out of heaven from God, prepared as a bride adorned for her husband. ... 22 [3] No longer will there be anything accursed, but the throne of God and of the Lamb will be in it, and his servants will worship him. ... [5] And night will be no more. They will need no light of lamp or sun, for the Lord God will be their light, and they will reign forever and ever.*

What kind of work do these verses describe: done by God? done by us?

God will create a new heaven and new earth (21:1); "prepare" the new Jerusalem "as a bride" (v 2); "wipe away every tear" (v 4); destroy death, mourning, crying and pain (v 4); "make all things new" (v 5). He will be the source of light in the new creation and reign with his people (22:5).

We will be God's servants (v 3) but also reign with him (v 5).

WATCH DVD 8.2 (6 min 26 sec) **OR DELIVER TALK 8.2** (see page 162)

* *Encourage the group to make notes as they watch the DVD or listen to the talk. There is space for notes on page 154 of the Handbook.*

Discuss

READ ISAIAH 65:17, 21-25

> ¹⁷ *"For behold, I create new heavens*
>   *and a new earth,*
> *and the former things shall not be remembered*
>   *or come into mind ...*
>
> ²¹ *"They shall build houses and inhabit them;*
>   *they shall plant vineyards and eat their fruit.*
> ²² *They shall not build and another inhabit;*
>   *they shall not plant and another eat;*
> *for like the days of a tree shall the days of my people be,*
>   *and my chosen shall long enjoy the work of their hands.*
> ²³ *They shall not labor in vain*
>   *or bear children for calamity,*
> *for they shall be the offspring of the blessed of the Lord,*
>   *and their descendants with them.*
> ²⁴ *Before they call I will answer;*
>   *while they are yet speaking I will hear.*
> ²⁵ *The wolf and the lamb shall graze together;*
>   *the lion shall eat straw like the ox,*
>   *and dust shall be the serpent's food.*

They shall not hurt or destroy
in all my holy mountain,"
says the LORD.

Isaiah 65 is the other key passage, alongside Revelation 21 and 22, that describes the new creation. What does Isaiah 65 tell us about work in the new creation?

- Work will *continue* in the new creation (Isaiah 65:21-22).
- Work will *be better* in the new creation (v 22-23).

NOTE: Isaiah's prophecy here has two horizons in view: the return of God's people from exile, back to the promised land; and the ultimate restoration of God's people to his promised land, in his new creation. We live between those two horizons. We can see that some parts of Isaiah 65 clearly apply to the promised land post-exile (eg: the existence of death, v 20)—though bear in mind this is an idealized depiction; the return from exile would prove to be disappointing, and leave God's people hungering for the further horizon of the new creation). Other parts apply to a creation restored to perfection (eg: the wolf and lamb, v 25). The purpose here is not to work out which horizon is in view at each point, but to appreciate the greatness of the new creation and the place of work within it.

The following table sums up what we have learned about work during this curriculum. Use the Bible passages to fill in the blanks.

CREATION	THE FALL	REDEMPTION	NEW CREATION
Genesis 2:15	Genesis 3:16-19	Romans 8:19-23	Isaiah 65:21-23
God created us to _____	Work was _____ by the fall	Work is being renewed and transformed by _____	Work will _____ and _____ in the new creation

The answers are:

| God created us to work | Work was marred/spoiled **by the fall** | Work is being **renewed and transformed by** the gospel | Work will continue **and** be better **in the new creation** |

▶ **WATCH DVD 8.3** (6 min 18 sec) **OR DELIVER TALK 8.3** (see page 162)

* *Encourage the group to make notes as they watch the DVD or listen to the talk. There is space for notes on page 156 of the Handbook.*

Discuss

In the DVD presentation, Tom says: **"We began in a garden, full of potential, called to work—and we will end in a city, full of potential, healed from the curse of the fall, and called to work as servants of the living God, and rulers with Christ in the new creation."**

How does the role of people in the Garden of Eden compare to our future role in the new creation?

The first people were put in the garden "to work it and keep it" (Genesis 2:15). They had been made in God's image and were to rule over every living thing (1:26-28). But this work was spoiled by the fall (3:16-19).

In the new creation, we are to work, including working the land (eg: "they shall plant vineyards and eat their fruit," Isaiah 65:21). We are to serve God (Revelation 22:3), and rule alongside God (v 5). This work will never be spoiled or be in vain (Isaiah 65:23).

How does knowing what we are looking forward to in the new creation help you when facing struggles with work today?

Remembering that we are heading to the new creation enables us to bear in mind that any problems we have with work today are temporary. This doesn't mean they aren't important, but it does mean that they won't last. We can look forward to a future where all work will be good and none will be in vain.

Look back over your notes and journal entries from the previous sessions.

- **What have you been encouraged by?**
- **What have you been particularly challenged by?**
- **What changes have you made as a result?**

Many of these sessions ended with an encouragement to make some changes in how we think and live. Ask people to look up what they wrote at the time, as well as anything they may have written in their weekly journal section.

If you have time, ask the group how they have been getting on with living out some of the action points from earlier in the course.

Pray

"Then I saw a new heaven and a new earth, for the first heaven and the first earth had passed away, and the sea was no more. And I saw the holy city, new Jerusalem, coming down out of heaven from God, prepared as a bride adorned for her husband. And I heard a loud voice from the throne saying, 'Behold, the dwelling place of God is with man. He will dwell with them, and they will be his people, and God himself will be with them as their God.'"

Ask God to help you serve him faithfully as you look forward to being with him in the new creation.

Look at some of the practical things you have written on this page. Pray that you will be able to put these into practice as you wait for the Lord to return.

DAILY BIBLE DEVOTIONALS

The final set of devotionals looks at Proverbs, highlighting what godly wisdom looks like when it comes to issues that affect the way we work day by day, such as laziness, honesty, integrity, speech, kindness and responding to injustice.

SERMONS

OPTION ONE: ISAIAH 65:21-25 / REVELATION 21 – 22

These passages were looked at by Tom in his presentation, and either (or all) could be expanded upon in a sermon.

OPTION TWO: PSALM 8

This is the passage the Bible study is based on (see next page), and could be preached as a great summary of the main themes of the whole curriculum (Note: Psalm 8 was the subject of the daily devotionals in Session 1).

OPTION THREE: 2 TIMOTHY 2:8-13

This passage sums up many of the underlying themes of this curriculum:
- When circumstances are hard, we must remember Jesus and therefore prioritize the showing and sharing of his word, for the good of his people (v 8-10).
- When circumstances are hard, we must rely on all that we have in Christ—a future of living and reigning with him for all his loyal subjects (v 11-13).

OPTION FOUR: GALATIANS 5:23 – SELF-CONTROL (AND, IF YOU MISSED OUT SESSION 7, GENTLENESS) AT WORK

Church members will find a page to write notes on the sermon on page 169 of their Handbooks.

BIBLE STUDY

AIM: If you have been using the Bible studies as part of this curriculum, this is probably the final thing you will do together. Use the opportunity both to sum up, and reinforce the main points from the series on how we are to think about and approach our working lives in the world. It might also be useful to ask if there are any unanswered questions that need to be thought about in the future. The main teaching session introduced us to the idea that the Bible sees eternity in the new creation as both physical (in resurrection bodies) and involving work, continuing to create, cultivate and co-operate as we fulfill God's creation command. This Bible study on Psalm 8 reinforces many of these points, but also asks us to think more deeply about our fundamental attitude toward ourselves and our work.

Discuss

If someone asked you to sum up the big ideas in *Gospel Shaped Work*, what would you tell them? Which have been the most surprising for you?

Allow the group to share the big ideas as they remember them. Encourage them to look back over their notes from previous weeks. Make sure that they do not just talk about themes of identity and ethics at work, but focus on the "big picture" theological truths about who God is (a worker) and how he is redeeming the world. It may be that people have reacted negatively to some ideas. Log them for discussion.

Gospel Shaped Work has laid out some powerful ideas that shine a very different light on our working lives, and our understanding as Christians. We've seen that:
- **God is revealed as a worker!**
- **God made us in his image as workers, and that work is good.**
- **Work has been frustrated by the fall.**
- **Christ not only redeemed his people through his death and resurrection, but in some way the whole world—our work will be redeemed in the new creation.**
- **In the new creation, we will continue to be workers—reigning with Christ and extending God's kingdom and glory into the whole of creation.**

In Psalm 8, we see some of these key ideas repeated.

READ PSALM 8

³ *When I look at your heavens, the work of your fingers,*
   the moon and the stars, which you have set in place,
⁴ *what is man that you are mindful of him,*
   and the son of man that you care for him?

1. **Verses 1-3 reveal God as a worker. How do we see the majesty of God's "name" (ie: his reputation) in what he has made?**

   - There is nothing more awesome than the night sky in all its glory. When we see it, we want to say: *"Wow!"*
   - Ask group members to share their experiences of how creation has moved them. It might not be just the big things (mountains, the ocean, the night sky), but also the small, intricate things—a flower, the structure of a cell or a snowflake under a microscope, or the hand of a newborn baby perhaps.
   - When we understand that there is a God who made the stars, the sun and the moon, we know that God is greater than all these things.
   - But the greatness and glory of God is also seen (v 2) in the weakest and most helpless thing, like a newborn baby. We get the same "wow" feeling when we see the astonishing miracle of a new child. The glorious sound of a crying baby is more powerful than the hate speech of God's enemies.

   Additional question: Do you routinely think of God as an active "worker" or as something else?

2. **What should these experiences of creation lead us to (v 1, 4)? What do the words used in verse 1 mean and imply?**

   - They should inspire us to praise and worship (serve) God.
   - "Majestic" implies kingship (from the title Majesty).
   - *O Lord*: the covenant name of God—*our Lord*—implies that we must personally put ourselves under the authority of the God of the covenant.
   - This is not just personal devotion to God. Praise always includes the element of making his name known to others. It's an obvious point, but the writer of Psalm 8 wrote a poem about it and got it published so that others would know! He wants the character and reputation for God to be known in "all the earth."
   - v 4: But not just praise at his greatness—there should also be a deep awareness of our own smallness and unworthiness in comparison.

3. **What position has God given to us in the world (v 5-8)? List the honors and responsibilities God has given to humankind.**

   - v 5: We are a little lower than the heavenly beings.
   - v 5: We are crowned with glory and honor.
   - v 6: We have been given dominion over the world.
   - v 6: Everything is "under [our] feet"—including the natural world of animals, birds and fish.

4. **What is the significance of the language used here—"dominion," "crowned," "under [our] feet"? How does v 4-6a help us keep a perspective on this privilege?**

   - This is the language of royalty. The LORD, the majestic King, has given to each of us the position of being a king in this world. We are rulers.
   - But our kingship is a privilege given to us in trust by God. We do not deserve it (v 4), but it is a gracious, generous gift.
   - We must always remember that what we are ruling is "the work of his hands" (v 6a). We rule it, but do not own it.

5. **How should these truths about our nature and position as people in God's world affect the way we view ourselves? How might it change the way we see others?**

   - We are incredibly privileged. We have been given the responsibility to rule the world, and to care for and steward God's precious creation.
   - This is something that *all* people have been given—irrespective of whether they call the LORD their Lord.
   - We should take our responsibility to rule seriously and humbly. We should create, co-operate and cultivate with seriousness, joy and determination.
   - We should recognize and value everyone because of their status.
   - We should honor, encourage and applaud anyone who rules—in their family, work, community, or in government—when they fulfill their creation mandate to create and cultivate co-operatively in a way that responsibly stewards God's creation. We can and should do this, even if they are not believers, or if part of what they are doing is flawed or driven by ungodly motives.

NOTE: There may be some in your group who find this idea difficult. We have a tendency to dismiss people entirely because they have a certain belief or a particular policy or attitude. We should be able to sift the good from the bad, and give praise for what honors God, even if other things are less praiseworthy in our estimation.

6. **Think about how you feel as you start work on a Monday morning. Think about common attitudes to work among your friends and colleagues. How might the perspective of Psalm 8 change our view of work—whatever that might be?**

- Our work, even if it is mundane and repetitive, can and must be viewed as worship. We are serving God in it and through it. The act of making a widget, changing a diaper, answering a call, sweeping a floor, planting a seed or sending an email can be—*in and of itself*—an act of worship when it is serving God's call to rule, order and cultivate the world, however we are feeling!
- It may not stop a job being difficult or dull, but invests it with new meaning. We can and should praise God for the privilege of our work, and strive to do it with joy and enthusiasm.
- We should also have a relentless positivity about the work of others. Even if they do not praise God in it, we can praise God *for* it.

Additional question: How can the ideas of us being "co-workers with God" now (Session 6), and our ultimate destiny as reigning co-workers in the new heavens and the new earth (Session 8) add to our thinking about our daily occupation?

READ HEBREWS 2:5-9

⁹ But we see him who for a little while was made lower than the angels, namely Jesus, crowned with glory and honor because of the suffering of death, so that by the grace of God he might taste death for everyone.

7. **The writer quotes Psalm 8. What is his assessment of where humanity as a whole has got to with this command to subdue the earth (see the contrast between v 8b and 8c)?**

"At present we do not see everything in subjection to him." Our test is incomplete. We still have a long way to go.

How has God ultimately fulfilled his own command to humanity (verse 9)?
Through Jesus. Jesus is the perfect man. Made lower than angels for a while,
he died for our sins, and rose again as Lord of all. He holds dominion over all
creation. Everything, even death, is "under his feet." The gospel of Jesus is the
fulfillment of God's creation command to the world.

Apply

FOR YOURSELF: Share with the group one big thing that you have been
challenged by during this course. How might you start—and continue—to
think and act differently as a result.

FOR YOUR CHURCH: How will you sustain the conversation in your
church, and the mutual encouragement about your daily work being part of
your godly calling and discipleship? How will you remind each other of the
truths we have uncovered during this course?

Pray

FOR YOUR GROUP: Pray through the things that people shared in the
Apply section above. Ask the Lord to help them change. But also ask the Lord
to help you encourage each other, and remind each other of gospel truths
about work when you are ground down by the difficulties and struggles of
working in a fallen world.

FOR YOUR CHURCH: Pray that you would be a church that is connected
to the world of work in an intelligent and compassionate way, and not a
church that is isolated and separate from it. Pray that your church would be
a place where all people are honored, respected and encouraged—whatever
their work. Pray that the fresh perspectives you have learned in this series
would remain alive in your group consciousness.

FURTHER READING

God will have work for us in heaven—and we ought to be glad for this! After all, if all we did in heaven was sit around with nothing to do, we'd get very bored.
Billy Graham

I have come home at last! This is my real country! I belong here. This is the land I have been looking for all my life, though I never knew it till now.
C.S. Lewis

There is a God, there is a future healed world that he will bring about, and your work is showing it (in part) to others. Your work will be only partially successful, on your best days, in bringing that world about. But inevitably ... beauty harmony, justice, comfort, joy and community will come to fruition.
Timothy Keller

Books

- Work Matters chapter four (Tom Nelson)
- Heaven (Randy Alcorn)
- Eternity Changes Everything (Stephen Witmer)

Online

- Rethinking Heaven: gospelshapedchurch.org/resources481
- The Basics of a Biblical Theology of Work: gospelshapedchurch.org/resources482
- The Justice Paradox (video): gospelshapedchurch.org/resources483

LEADER'S REFLECTIONS

MORE RESOURCES
TO HELP SHAPE YOUR
WORK

Connecting **Sunday worship** to **Monday work**

Work. For some this word represents drudgery and the mundane. For others work is an idol to be served. If you find yourself anywhere on the spectrum from workaholic to weekend warrior, it's time to bridge the gap between Sunday worship and Monday work.

Striking a balance between theological depth and practical counsel, Tom Nelson outlines God's purposes for work in a way that helps us to make the most of our vocation and to join God in his work in the world. Discover a new perspective on work that will transform your workday and make the majority of your waking hours matter, not only now, but for eternity.

TOM NELSON is Senior Pastor of Christ Community Church in Leawood, Kansas, and President of the Made to Flourish network.

WWW.CROSSWAY.ORG

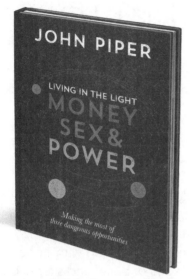

What, or who, is at the center of your universe? John Piper shows us the blazing glory of Christ and urges us to set him as the sun at the center of our personal solar systems, so that each area of our life might orbit in the way it was designed to.

When Christ is our supreme treasure, we are able to keep money, sex and power in their proper place, enjoying them and glorifying God with them instead of rejecting them or worshiping them.

JOHN PIPER is founder and teacher of desiringGod Ministries and chancellor of Bethlehem College and Seminary. He is author of more than 50 books.

Christopher Ash, from his own experience, knows what burnout looks and feels like. He reveals a neglected biblical truth and seven keys that flow from it. Understood properly, and built into our lives as Christians who are zealous to serve the Lord, they will serve to protect us from burnout, and keep us working for God's kingdom and glory.

CHRISTOPHER ASH
is a Pastor and author.

WWW.THEGOODBOOK.COM

LIVE | GROW | KNOW

Live with Christ, Grow in Christ, Know more of Christ.

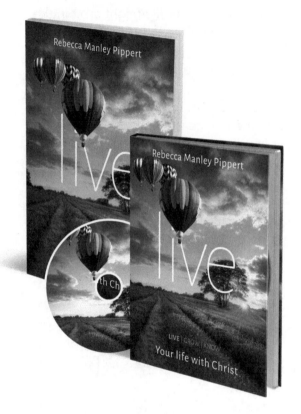

"These studies by Becky Pippert are clear and accessible, yet substantial and thoughtful explorations of how to be grounded and grow in Christian faith. They evidence years of experience working with people at all stages of belief and skepticism. I highly recommend them."

Tim Keller

PART **1**

live

Explores what the Christian life is like.

Ever got to the end of running an evangelistic course and wondered: What next?

LiveGrowKnow is a brand new series from globally-renowned speaker Rebecca Manley Pippert, designed to help people continue their journey from enquirer to disciple to mature believer.

Part 1, Live, consists of five DVD-based sessions and is the perfect follow-up to an evangelistic course or event, or for anyone who wants to explore the Christian life more deeply.

REBECCA MANLEY PIPPERT
Globally-renowned speaker and author of
Out of the Saltshaker

PART **2**

grow

Explores how we
mature as Christians.

I'm a Christian… what next?
These studies show what God's plan for
our lives is, and how we can get going
and get growing in the Christian life.

For groups who have done the LIVE
course, GROW is the follow-up; it also
works perfectly as a stand-alone course
for groups wishing to think about how
to grow in a real and exciting way.
Handbook and DVD available.

PART **3**

know

Looks at core
doctrines of the faith.

WWW.THEGOODBOOK.COM/LGK

GOSPEL SHAPED

CHURCH

The Complete Series

**LET THE POWER OF THE GOSPEL SHAPE
FOUR OTHER CRITICAL AREAS IN THE LIFE
OF YOUR CHURCH**

> **"WE WANT CHURCHES CALLED INTO EXISTENCE BY THE GOSPEL TO BE SHAPED BY THE GOSPEL IN THEIR EVERYDAY LIFE."**

DON CARSON AND TIM KELLER

GOSPEL SHAPED
WORSHIP

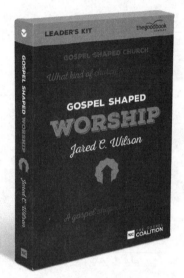

Christians are people who have discovered that the one true object of our worship is the God who has revealed himself in and through Jesus Christ.

But what exactly is worship? What should we be doing when we meet together for "church" on Sundays? And how does that connect with what we do the rest of the week?

This seven-week whole-church curriculum explores what it means to be a worshiping community. As we search the Scriptures together, we will discover that true worship must encompass the whole of life. This engaging and flexible resource will challenge us to worship God every day of the week, with all our heart, mind, soul and strength.

Written and presented by **JARED C. WILSON**
Jared is Director of Communications at Midwestern Seminary and College in Kansas City, and a prolific author. He is married to Becky and has two daughters.

WWW.GOSPELSHAPEDCHURCH.ORG/WORSHIP

GOSPEL SHAPED
OUTREACH

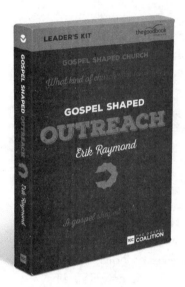

Many Christians are nervous about telling someone else about Jesus. The nine sessions in this curriculum don't offer quick fixes or evangelism "gimmicks." But by continually pointing us back to the gospel, they will give us the proper motivation to work together as a church to share the gospel message with those who are lost without Christ.

As you work through the material, you will discover that God's mission of salvation in the world is also your mission; and that he is inviting you into the privilege of praying and working to advance his kingdom among your family, friends, neighbors, co-workers and community.

Gospel Shaped Church is a new curriculum from The Gospel Coalition that will help whole congregations pause and think slowly, carefully and prayerfully about the kind of church they are called to be.

Written and presented by **ERIK RAYMOND**
Erik is the Preaching Pastor at Emmaus Bible Church in Omaha, Nebraska. He is married to Christie and has six children.

WWW.GOSPELSHAPEDCHURCH.ORG/OUTREACH

GOSPEL SHAPED
LIVING

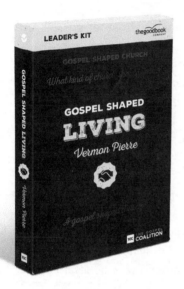

Start a fresh discussion in your church about how the gospel of Christ impacts every area of life in our world.

Gospel Shaped Living is a track that explores over seven sessions what it means for a local church to be a distinctive, counter-cultural community.

Through the gospel, God calls people from every nation, race and background to be joined together in a new family that shows his grace and glory. How should our lives as individuals and as a church reflect and model the new life we have found in Christ? And how different should we be to the world around us?

This challenging and interactive course will inspire us to celebrate grace and let the gospel shape our lives day by day.

Written and presented by **VERMON PIERRE**
Vermon is the Lead Pastor of Roosevelt Community Church in Phoenix, Arizona. He is married to Dennae and has three children.

WWW.GOSPELSHAPEDCHURCH.ORG/LIVING

> "THESE RESOURCES GIVE SPACE TO CONSIDER WHAT A GENUINE EXPRESSION OF A GOSPEL-SHAPED CHURCH LOOKS LIKE FOR YOU IN THE PLACE GOD HAS PUT YOU, AND WITH THE PEOPLE HE HAS GATHERED INTO FELLOWSHIP WITH YOU."

DON CARSON AND TIM KELLER

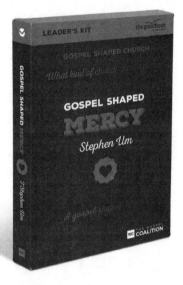

GOSPEL SHAPED
MERCY

The gospel is all about justice and mercy: the just punishment of God falling on his Son, Jesus, so that he can have mercy on me, a sinner.

But many churches have avoided following through on the Bible's clear teaching on working for justice and mercy in the wider world. They fear that it is a distraction from the primary task of gospel preaching.

This *Gospel Shaped Mercy* module explores how individual Christians and whole churches can and should be engaged in the relief of poverty, hunger and injustice in a way that adorns the gospel of grace.

Written and presented by **STEPHEN UM**
Stephen is Senior Minister of Citylife Church in Boston, MA, and is a council member of The Gospel Coalition.

WWW.GOSPELSHAPEDCHURCH.ORG/MERCY

thegoodbook
COMPANY

Opening up the Bible

At The Good Book Company, we are dedicated to helping Christians and local churches grow. We believe that God's growth process always starts with hearing clearly what he has said to us through his timeless word—the Bible.

Ever since we opened our doors in 1991, we have been striving to produce resources that honor God in the way the Bible is used. We have grown to become an international provider of user-friendly resources to the Christian community, with believers of all backgrounds and denominations using our Bible studies, books, evangelistic resources, DVD-based courses and training events.

We want to equip ordinary Christians to live for Christ day by day, and churches to grow in their knowledge of God, their love for one another, and the effectiveness of their outreach.

Call us for a discussion of your needs or visit one of our local websites for more information on the resources and services we provide.

North America: www.thegoodbook.com
UK & Europe: www.thegoodbook.co.uk
Australia: www.thegoodbook.com.au
New Zealand: www.thegoodbook.co.nz

North America: 866 244 2165
UK & Europe: 0333 123 0880
Australia: (02) 6100 4211
New Zealand (+64) 3 343 2463